HIDDEN HISTORY *of* ANDERSON COUNTY

Liz Carey

FOREWORD BY KATHRYN SMITH

THE History PRESS

Published by The History Press
Charleston, SC
www.historypress.net

Front cover: National Archives.
Back cover, top: author's collection; *bottom*: Library of Congress.

First published 2018

Manufactured in the United States

ISBN 9781467136709

Library of Congress Control Number: 2017958373

Contents

Contents

Foreword

I often say that researching history is like lowering a bucket into a moving river. When you drop your bucket in, you never know what you will haul out. Liz Carey has dipped her bucket into the history of Anderson County many times with this book, *Hidden History of Anderson County*. Once you read it, you will never look at your community with the same eyes. Who knew what a rich history we have, of the leaders and misleaders, schemers and dreamers, doers and un-doers, who made Anderson County what it is today.

Starting way back in colonial days, Liz tells you about how the Cherokee Indians, this county's original habitants, lost out by backing the wrong side in the Revolutionary War. Moving ahead into the Civil War era, she relates the fascinating story of how the Yankees who rode into Anderson in search of the Confederate gold were diverted by free wine—thanks to a quick-thinking judge.

One of the most amazing little-known stories she shares is the sensational "Trial of the Nineteenth Century," which literally changed the course of justice in Reconstruction South Carolina—and directly led to the impeachment of President Andrew Johnson.

That was only one case of local people interacting with movers and shakers on the national stage. How fascinating to learn that William Church Whitner took the side of a brilliant underdog electrical engineer who was warring with the celebrated Thomas Edison about the best way to deliver electrical current to the masses. Whitner met Nicola Tesla, adopted his alternating current method, successfully transmitted electricity six miles from a power plant on the Seneca River to Anderson's streetlights and, as a result, Anderson got its honorific, "The Electric City," in 1895.

Another Anderson entrepreneur, Alton P. Durham, studied with the brilliant scientist George Washington Carver and went on to develop his stomach medicine, Vim Herb.

Anderson escaped the worst ravages of the Civil War, but in July 1941, five months before Pearl Harbor, it was captured in one minute by the enemy forces of Clemsonia.

Once you've read this book, I'm sure you will go searching your county for evidence of these and other stories: the lonely grave of Maud Broadwick, the first woman killed in an aerial accident in South Carolina; the monuments to Amelia Earhart's flight here in 1931 and the seven Honea Path textile workers who lost their lives in the bloody labor riot of 1934; and the former women's school that briefly housed the Confederate treasury in the last days of the Civil War.

Sit down with this book, take a dipper into the bucket of history and be prepared to be fascinated.

—Kathryn Smith, author of *The Gatekeeper: Missy LeHand, FDR, and the Untold Story of the Partnership that Defined a Presidency*

Acknowledgements

This book would not have been possible if it hadn't been for many, many people who have helped me and inspired me along the way.

A big thank-you to Alison Hinman, former curator of the Anderson County Museum, who started me on a path of learning more about Anderson County and its history. From ballooning accidents, to riots, to drunken Union troops, many of the stories I learned from the museum and from Alison were hard to believe, until I did the research. And the research was fascinating. A big thank-you to Brian Scott, whose knowledge of Anderson and the surrounding area astounds me daily. And my heartfelt appreciation goes out to Pam Christopher, who forwarded me an e-mail from someone looking for just such a book as this. Some of Brian's stories were the inspiration to do more research into events in Anderson through the years as well.

Dan Cooper, who served as one of my readers, helped me not only as a fact checker, but also as an ever-present grammar Nazi, keeping my head in the game when it came to clear and concise writing. Special thanks to Jennifer Norman, who is not only my favorite lunch date but also the one who listened to me whine, moan, complain, gush and kibitz over the past year and a half—sometimes even about the book. To those who held me accountable, one note at a time, throughout this process, I am eternally grateful.

And thanks as well to my family and friends, most especially Mason Carey, Mason Robert Carey, Max Carey, Hannah Wellborn, Phyllis Carey,

Kathy Hogg, Steve Hogg, Matt Schell, Kathy Mulz, Tammy Ramsey, Rusty Ramsey, Missy Cooper and Melba Cooper, all of whom helped me to stay focused, stay on target and stay confident that I could do it.

Introduction

Anderson County has been home to people since the thirteenth century. First, as part of the Cherokee Nation, then as a key part of the Revolutionary War, then, later, as a refuge from the malaria and heat of the South Carolina coast and, later still, as a key part of the modernization of the South, Anderson has held a place in South Carolina history for centuries.

These stories are taken from the pages of history—from news accounts, written stories and historical records—to illustrate some of the lesser-known facts about Anderson County, its municipalities and the people who call this community home.

Many of these stories I questioned when I heard about them the first time. I'm sure there are some that will leave you scratching your head, too.

But all of them come from qualified sources and have been checked against the actual records as they exist.

Part I

COLONIAL TIMES

I

Indian Lands of the Creek and Cherokee

As far back as the early 1200s, there have been people on this land. Indians—Cherokee, Chippewa and Creek—lived in this area well before the white man came. In the 1500s, the land was divided into five Cherokee states or towns: Overhill Town, Valley Town, Middle Town, Lower Town and Out Town. Lower Towns stretched from what is now Cherokee, North Carolina, to Franklin, North Carolina, to the South Carolina Upstate and down to Columbia.

In 1539, Hernando de Soto and his Spanish explorers came inland and visited the Lower Towns area. The capital then was Keowee. Translated literally from the Cherokee, it means "Place of the Mulberries." Indians hunted and fished the land and grew corn, their primary crop and food source. Fish were often used as fertilizer for cornstalks. For meat, the Cherokees hunted deer, buffalo, turkey, bear, wild boar and other small game.

Unlike the traditional depiction of Indians, the Cherokees lived in log houses. They foraged through the woods for roots, tree bark and leaves to use in healing. And they ground their corn into a mush, which was oftentimes fried or eaten as a stew.

In 1670, the British established Carolina as a colony. Once they came, trade between the British and the Native Americans was established. Opportunity flourished—for the white men, especially. Indians traded furs and vegetables to the British, and in return, the British provided them with weapons, glass beads, bells, woven blankets and alcohol. In turn, the British

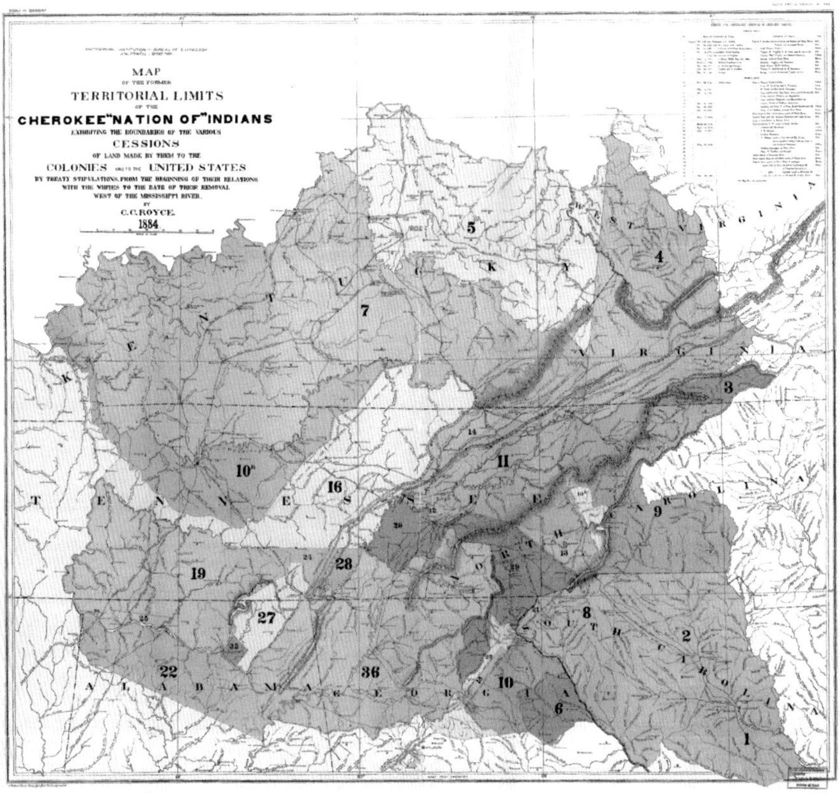

A map of the Cherokee Nation, circa 1884. *Library of Congress.*

sold the furs to the French and others, who used the furs in hats, coats and other products.

By 1753, Royal Governor James Glen approached the Cherokee chiefs and displayed British friendship by saying the royal government would build a fort across the river from Keowee to protect the Cherokees from the Creek Indians. In reality, Glen was building the fort to protect the British from the Cherokees.

By the late 1750s, fur trade had diminished, as fashions began to change. The Cherokees felt cheated when their relationship with the English waned. Around the same time, several Cherokee deaths occurred at the hands of the British, leaving the Cherokees with a sour taste in their mouths for the English. Finally, in 1759, the Cherokees decide to wage war against the British.

In the beginning of their relationship, in the mid-1750s, the Cherokee Nation had sided with the British during the French and Indian War. British generals had intelligence that the French were planning to build forts in Cherokee territory, which they shared with the Cherokee. Once the Cherokees agreed to work with the British troops, the British immediately built forts of their own in Cherokee lands—most notably Fort Prince George.

Once the forts were built, the Cherokees raised close to seven hundred warriors to fight in western Virginia and another group of warriors to attack the French at Fort Toulouse. In 1758, the Cherokees helped the British in the taking of Fort Duquesne (now known as Pittsburgh). On their way home, however, several missteps and mistakes led to conflict between the Cherokees and the British. The Cherokee men had been promised supplies in exchange for their fighting efforts. But there was a misunderstanding as to where they were to get them. Thinking that they had arrived at the supply location, the Indians took some horses they believed were rightly theirs. When they did, several Virginians came after them and scalped between thirty and forty of them.

At first, many Cherokee leaders called for peace. But others took action, leading retaliatory raids on pioneer settlements. South Carolina governor William Henry Lyttleton made his stand. He stopped all shipments of gunpowder to the Cherokees and raised an army of 1,100 men to confront the Cherokees in the Lower Towns. Desperate for ammunition, the Cherokee Nation sent a delegation of moderate chiefs to Lyttleton to negotiate. All 29 chiefs were taken hostage and sent to Fort Prince George. Lyttleton felt the hostages would ensure peace with the Cherokee Nation. Instead, it incensed the Indians, who continued to attack settlements into 1760.

In February of that year, the Indians attacked Fort Prince George in an effort to rescue their hostages. In the process, they killed the fort's commander. His replacement ordered the immediate execution of the hostages. Instead of being calmed, the Cherokees retaliated more. With attacks into North Carolina as far east as modern-day Winston-Salem and as close as Fort Ninety Six, the Indians were able to overthrow several villages.

Lyttleton turned to Jeffrey Amherst, the British commander in North America, for help. Amherst sent Archibald Montgomerie with an army of 1,200 troops to South Carolina. The troops razed the Lower Towns, including Keowee.

In 1761, Montgomerie was replaced by James Grant. Grant led an army of 2,600 men to fight the Cherokees. The army moved through the Lower

Towns and proceeded to raze other Cherokee states, burning fields and crops as they went.

In the end, the Cherokees surrendered and, ultimately, on the advice of British commissioner Andrew Cameron, pledged their loyalty to "Our father, the King of England." It would put them on the wrong side of the coming Revolutionary War. Because of their allegiance to England, the Cherokees sided with the British and those loyal to the British government in the Revolutionary War. On July 1, 1776, the Cherokees joined in attacks against Revolutionary forces.

At the time, Major Andrew Williamson was raising rebel troops to fight the British. His forces gathered at Ninety Six on July 2. A few days later, he had 110 men gathered at DeWitt's Corner, now Due West, on the edge of the Indian lands. By the end of the month, Williamson's company totaled more than 1,100 men. Traveling down the ridge from Six and Twenty Creek, the rebels set up a base came. It had taken them more than three weeks to travel sixty miles. Their camp was located north of Anderson, near where Interstate 85 crosses U.S. 76.

Just before August, Williamson and his men picked up thirty horsemen and crossed the valley of 18 Mile Creek to attack Seneca Village (not the city of Seneca we know today). With Williamson leading the group and Captain Andrew Pickens of Long Cane and his men in the rear, the group staked out a camp on the edge of the village. Williamson's men stood ready to fight at the fence line surrounding the village.

Suddenly, the men were attacked by Indians and British troops dressed as Indians. The group opened fire on the rebels. Ten or twelve of Williamson's militiamen died immediately. But Williamson continued the battle. Pickens organized his men to move forward. The Indians took to the trees and continued to fire on the rebel troops until at last they retreated.

In retaliation, Williamson's forces struck the Cherokee settlement of Sinica (again, not to be confused with Seneca Village, or the modern-day Seneca) and burned it to the ground. Men provisioned for themselves and then destroyed whatever crops were left, leaving the Indians with nothing. Turning their backs to the Indian village, the forces moved on to the next Cherokee encampment and attacked. Williamson and his remaining 640 men marched along the Oconee, the Tugaloo and the Osttaloy Rivers, destroying villages as they went.

By August 11, Williamson had joined forces with others in the Upstate and attacked settlements of Indians and British sympathizers alike all through what is now the Greenville area. They moved on to Fort Prince

George, destroying every town as they went. Once again, they met up with Captain Pickens, who had joined with his friend Captain Robert Anderson to search for the enemy. When they found them, they killed them. More than sixteen Indians died in the conflict in hand-to-hand combat.

A month later, with a combined force of 2,300, now-Colonel Williamson moved deeper into Cherokee lands in the Middle Towns, near Columbia. By October, the Cherokees had been defeated. The war had taken its toll. Some 99 militiamen were dead, but more than 2,000 Indians had died during the conflict.

The Indians looked to their advisor, Commissioner Andrew Cameron, for guidance. But Cameron was nowhere to be found. When fighting started, Cameron had moved to Florida to escape from harm.

Following the Revolutionary War, South Carolina became a state and was divided into districts. By 1789, Pendleton District was created on former Indian lands. The county included what is now Anderson and Pickens Counties. It also included all but seventy square miles of land along the Chattooga River in Oconee County that belonged to the Cherokee and Creek Indian tribes.

By this time, Pendleton was becoming quite famous for its rolling hills, mountain views and thriving trade center. Residents of plantations on the coast came to Pendleton to vacation during the summer, avoiding the heat of the beach as well as the deadly malaria.

2

Pendleton District to Anderson County and Farmers Hall

In 1791, the Pendleton District was dissolved and incorporated into the Washington Equity Court District, which included what is now Greenville, Anderson, Pickens and Oconee Counties. At first, the district seat and courthouse were in Rockville, but friends of then-General Andrew Pickens successfully petitioned to change the name to Pickensville. The little courthouse and village were located on the town's main thoroughfare, Federal Street, which was crossed by Pinckney Street, named after the owner of the land the town was located on, Governor Charles Pinckney.

Just nine years later, Pendleton District was reestablished, and the courthouse was moved to the city of Pendleton. Sadly, although it was once the site of a military muster grounds, Pickensville disappeared as the years passed. The small jail built in the village was in bad repair, and when the residents of the Pendleton District built their own jail, the main courthouse was housed in Pendleton as well. In 1815, a fire broke out in the town. There was enough property loss that a lottery was approved to help residents who had lost property due to the fire. The lottery was a bust, however, because the operators accepted promise notes instead of cash for tickets and were not able to collect on the promises. Later that year, the entire town was sold, except for a few lots.

In 1825, Robert Mills described the town as containing:

> *a court-house and jail, a Presbyterian and Episcopal church, 40 houses, several of them neat, an academy, printing office, (issuing a weekly paper,)*

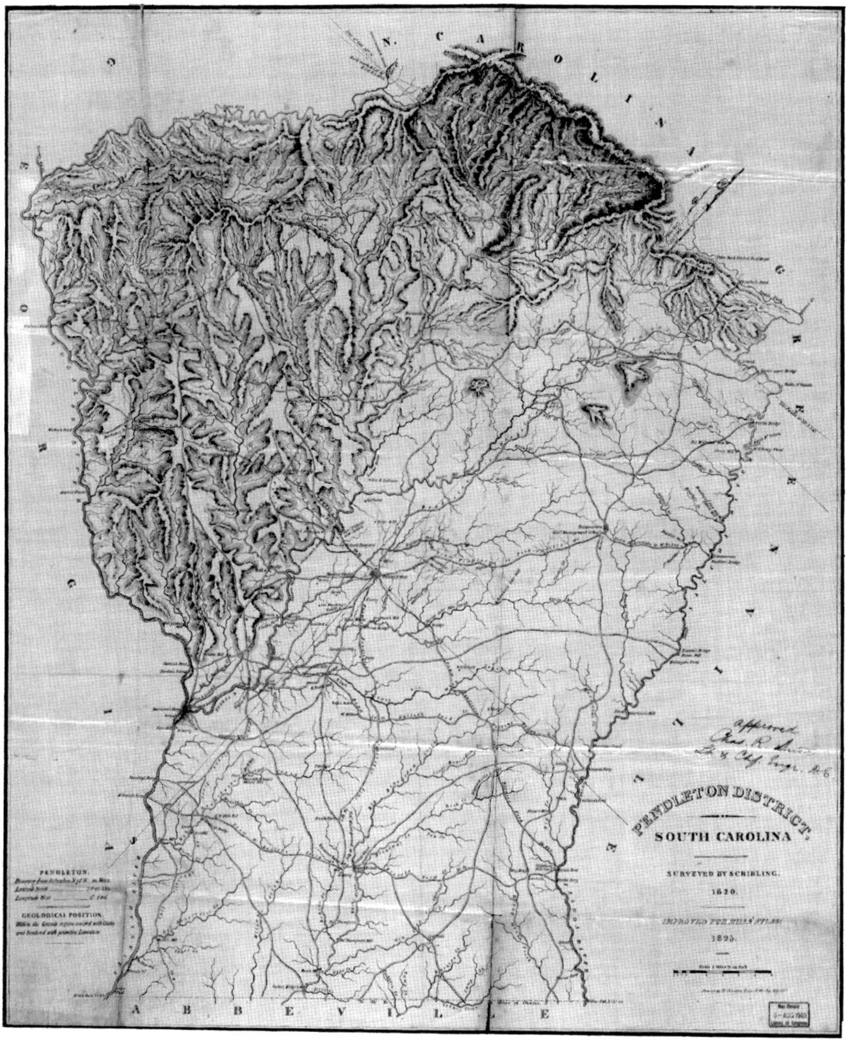

Pendleton District, circa 1820. *Library of Congress.*

and an agricultural hall, for the meeting of a society of this nature. There is every prospect of the village increasing in population. A very select society is found here, and in the neighborhood, where some gentlemen of fortune and high respectability, from the low country, have located themselves and families.

In 1826, the Pendleton District was dissolved. In its stead came the Anderson and Pickens Districts, the former named after Revolutionary War hero Robert Anderson. By 1828, the town of Anderson had become Anderson Courthouse, and its residents built a courthouse. The county seat then moved from the city of Pendleton to the city of Anderson Courthouse. At the time, a second courthouse and jail were under construction in Pendleton. The building was finished by the Pendleton Farmers' Society and is still standing. It is known as Farmers Hall.

Behind Farmers Hall, the Hunter's Store stands today as one of the oldest buildings in Pendleton. Originally a blacksmith shop and then a general store, Hunter's Store was built in 1850. Today, it serves as the visitor's center and offices for the Pendleton District Commission.

James Hunter erected the building in the 1850s as a blacksmith shop. In 1870, he began operating a store with a Mr. Long, and it was known as Hunter and Long. The two-story building was located on Queen Street, where it still stands. Hunter bought out Long in 1873 and began running the store as James Hunter—Dealer in General Merchandise. As his family grew, he incorporated his two sons, James T. Hunter and Miles M. Hunter, into the store as James Hunter and Sons.

When the senior James Hunter died in 1889, his sons continued to run the business as a general store. Miles Hunter eventually bought his brother

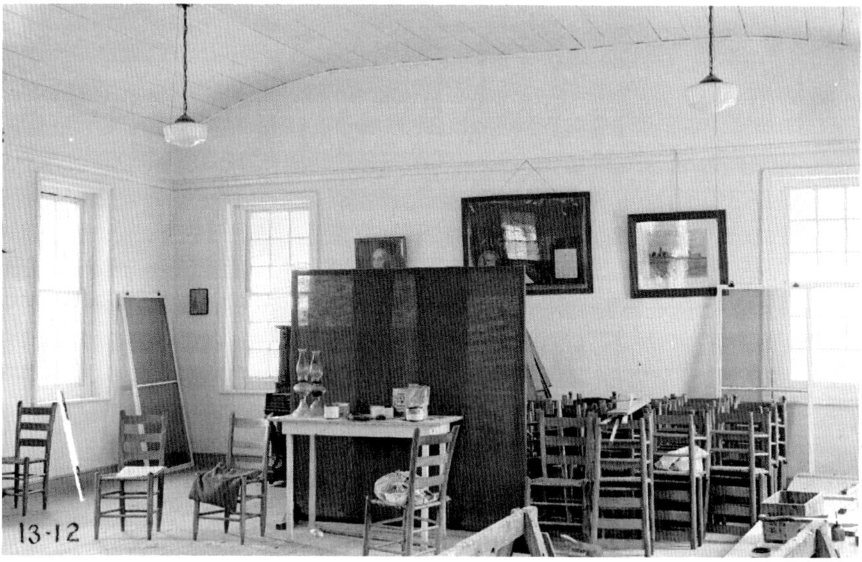

An interior shot of Farmers Hall during construction, circa 1934. *Library of Congress.*

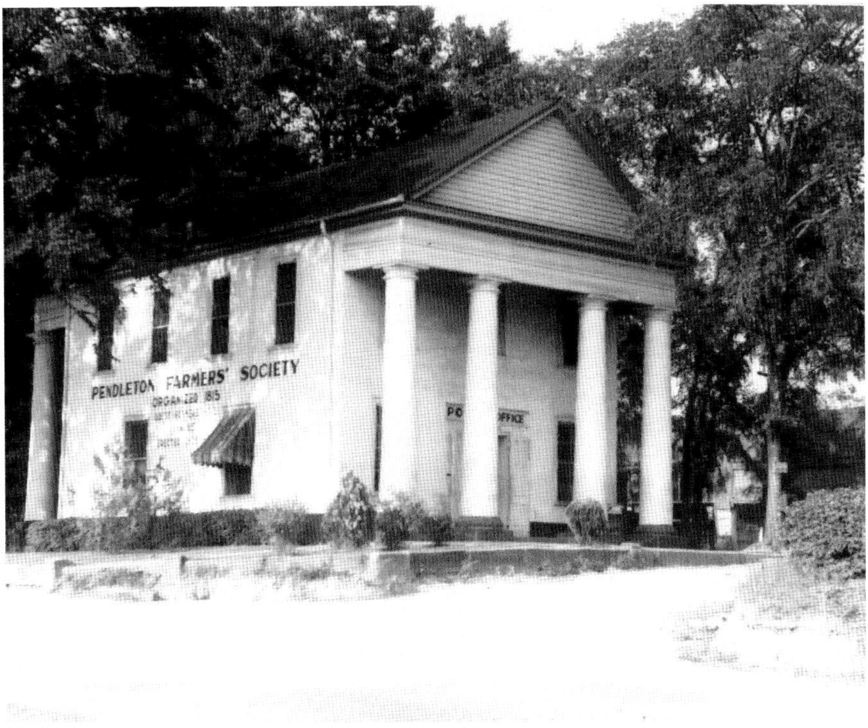

Farmers Hall. *Library of Congress.*

out and ran the store as MM Hunter—General Merchandise, Fertilizers and Cotton. About 1916, he changed the name to MM Hunter—General Merchandise and Cotton.

In 1929, another building was erected across the street. It became the store, while the original store became a warehouse of sorts. This new store ran until 1962, operated after the death of Miles by his sons Benjamin Gaillard Hunter, Ralph Hunter and Miles Hunter. When the sons closed the store, the assets were liquidated and the building closed.

The Pendleton District Commission purchased the original Hunter's Store in 1967. Today, it serves as a depository for historic records, including some of the original records from Hunter's Store, such as customer invoices, charge accounts and correspondence.

On the second floor of Hunter's Store, just inside the doorway on the doorframe, a wooden beam is marked with names carved into it. About halfway up the frame, the words "Very cold" may be what some believe are the last words of a dead man who it's said still haunts Hunter's Store.

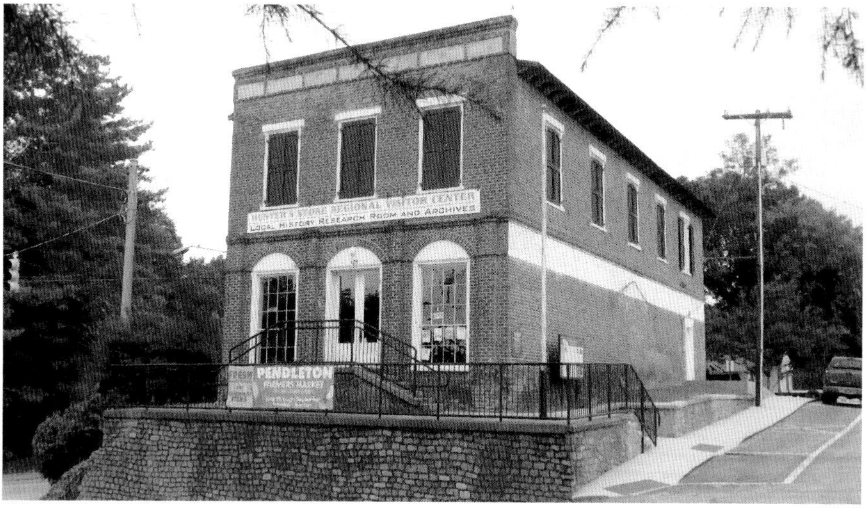

Hunter's Store in Pendleton now serves as home to the Pendleton District Commission. *Author's collection.*

As the story goes, in the late 1800s, when the Hunter brothers ran the store, a man was riding home a little inebriated. Because of his condition, he fell off his horse and into 18 Mile Creek. The brothers, hoping to save the man from the wrath of his wife, let him stay in the store in the caretaker's quarters. They put him, in his soaking wet clothes, upstairs on a cot. It had been a warm day, and they felt he would be okay enough to dry off and sober up.

But that night, the temperatures dropped below freezing. When the brothers returned the next morning, the man had died of exposure.

Some say his ghost still haunts the store. There have been reports of unexplained noises, shadowy figures and the sound of scurrying footsteps. Those who've seen the ghost say the feeling they get when he is around is cold and unfriendly.

3
The General's Road

In the late 1700s, General Andrew Pickens blazed a trail that is still in use today—the General's Road.

Running from Pendleton to Abbeville, the road was used to travel between districts as well as to connect with other roads leading to the coast. Pickens and General Robert Anderson both owned property along the road, and it is still the location of some of the county's oldest and most architecturally significant homes.

It is likely that farmers from North Carolina would have used the General's Road while driving their cattle and hogs to market. At that time, tourists and merchants would have traveled from Asheville to the Pendleton District on the Buncombe Turnpike, which connected to the General's Road. Farmers who lived in the Pendleton District would have sold their produce to the travelers.

Another frequent traveler of the road was John C. Calhoun. Along the way, the travelers may have stopped at Varennes. This was the name given to a township just south of Anderson. The word is French for "wasteland." Farther south, Abbeville was settled by French Huguenots and probably referred to that area (on the edge of the Indian territory) as the white man's wasteland.

The township was named after the church built there in the 1800s, as well as a school. The current Varennes Elementary School was named after the original township. For a while, Varennes was the social hub of the area, especially Varennes Tavern.

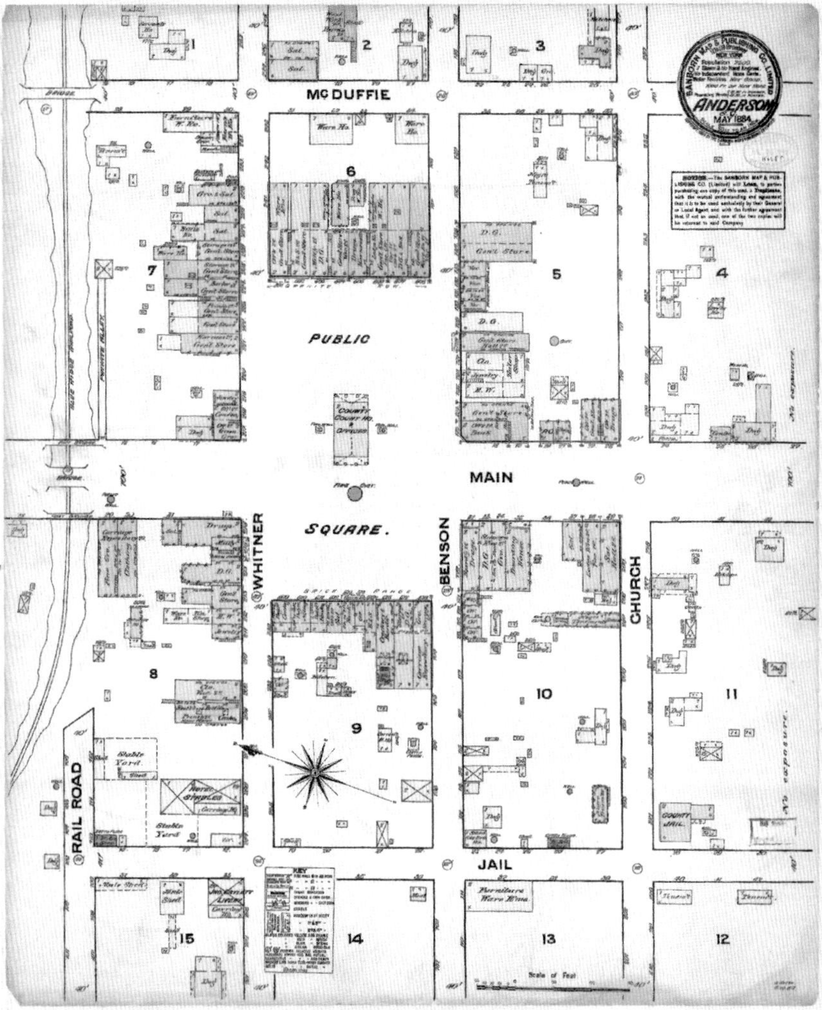

Anderson city map, 1844. *South Carolina Department of Archives and History.*

Also along the General's Road was Craytonville. Standing at the crossroads of Anderson and Honea Path, Craytonville was once a thriving community. Located inside the town was Orr's Tavern. According to legend, a widow, Ann Hanks, bought the tavern, and worked it with her son and daughter, Nancy.

The story goes that, one day in 1809, a hog drover named Thomas Lincoln showed up in the Pendleton District. After selling the hogs, he

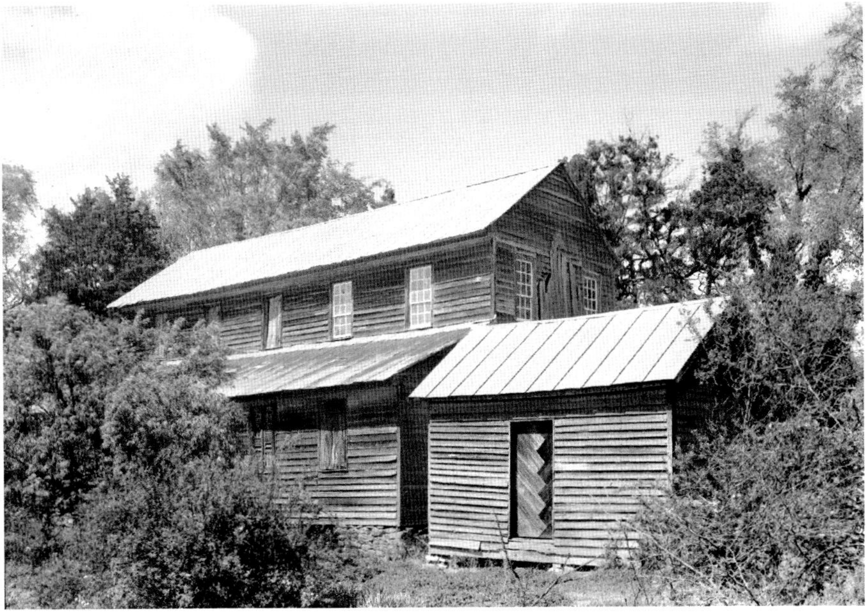

Varennes Tavern along the General's Road. *Library of Congress.*

stayed on in Craytonville to look after a farm for an absentee landowner. Sometime after, he decided to return to his native Kentucky with his new bride, Nancy Hanks. Yes, that Nancy Hanks—mother of Abraham Lincoln.

Now, there is an even shadier legend that says Nancy Hanks was also seeing John C. Calhoun at the time; but, because he was married, she couldn't let anyone know. The legend says that she found herself in a "family way" and opted to wed Lincoln and leave the state rather than embarrass Calhoun. Theorists say that this could explain why Calhoun and Abraham Lincoln look so much alike.

There are tales of another tavern along the General's Road. This tavern, however, had a much darker history. According to those legends, there were three siblings, one brother and two sisters, the Moores, who ran their own tavern on the General's Road. The girls' names were Rachel and Sarah. Because they were on a well-traveled road, they often took in travelers, grabbing their cases and belongings from the wagons or horses that went by. Often, however, these travelers were never seen or heard from again.

When Rachel got in trouble with local law enforcement, she was hauled into court. There, she promptly spat on the judge. The two sisters ran away from the tavern in the middle of the night, eager to avoid any more interaction with the local constabulary.

The tavern sat empty for years. Later, when someone bought the property, the new owners were clearing up the place when they cleaned out the well. Inside the well, they found several human bones. Could they have been the remains of the lost travelers?

The General's Road remained a popular thoroughfare throughout the nineteenth and twentieth centuries. Eventually, part of the road became known as Clemson Boulevard; the rest became the Abbeville Highway. The road travels along South Carolina 28 and then through the Anderson Historic District on Boulevard and then on Main Street until it turns into Clemson Boulevard. When one looks from the road up to the outskirts of the Blue Ridge Mountains, one can see why it has always been such a popular thoroughfare.

4
Andersonville

More than a quarter of a century before the city of Anderson was laid out, a small port on the Savannah River was the center of industry for the area.

Located where the Tugaloo and the Seneca Rivers meet, Andersonville was a booming town on the western edges of the Pendleton District. Established in 1792, the town grew as a destination along the river, providing cities south and west of it with cotton. It was said to be bigger, at the time, than Anderson or Pendleton.

In 1801, the South Carolina legislature certified the town on land owned by one of the settlers of the Upstate, Colonel Elias Earle. Earle sold off a few pieces of the land and then gave part of it to his son-in-law, James Harrison. Earle had been a military officer in the Revolutionary War and afterward served as a member of Congress. Harrison went on to build a business on the river's edge.

The town had a flour mill and a gristmill, a cotton gin, a clock factory, a cotton factory, a wool factory, a tailor shop, a shoe shop, a livery stable, an iron foundry and an academy for young women. There was even a forty-room hotel to accommodate the travelers who came to Andersonville from the river.

Later, during the Civil War, the town supposedly supported a factory that made yarn from cottonseed—likely the only such one in the South.

It was said that John C. Calhoun would frequent Andersonville to find the best river pilots. He questioned them about the feasibility of his idea to open the Savannah for transportation by increasing its depth.

The town was an important place for trade along the river. Boats loaded with cotton were sent from Andersonville to Hamburg and Augusta, Georgia. James Harrison was said to have bought more than six hundred bales of cotton and ground more than twenty thousand bushels of wheat per year, a pretty substantial amount for the time. According to the National Register of Historic Places, the town also supported the Indian trade of selling pinkroot, snakeroot and ginseng down the river.

During the War of 1812, Elias Earle secured a contract with the federal government to manufacture muskets on the island. Earle, with the help of thirty-two machinists brought in from Harpers Ferry, Virginia, built an armory on Andersonville and started making the weapons. Unfortunately, the area wasn't good for making iron. Earle's muskets were known to be dangerous. The guns would burst, making them more of a hazard to the shooter than the target.

Still, the town flourished, with two ferries going back and forth over the Tugaloo River and Beaver Creek to reach it. In 1840, however, the water that brought Andersonville its fame ultimately also took it away. A freshet, or flood caused by heavy rains, carried away the cotton gin, cotton mill and wool mill. They were rebuilt, but river floods carried them away again in 1852. It was the beginning of the end for the bustling town.

As the Greenville and Columbia Railroad came to Anderson, the river town of Andersonville began its slow death spiral. Although there were moves to add a spur of the railroad line to reach Andersonville, it never happened. Railroad travel and trade replaced the river, and Andersonville lost its importance in the area. But it was still a place people wanted to go. In 1885, a story in the *Anderson Intelligencer* reminisced about Andersonville and its glory days.

> [E]*arly in the morning the caravan of picknickers* [sic] *began to wend its way toward Andersonville, SC, distant nine miles. Mr. Robert Stephenson and ourself* [sic] *"went in together" and procured a conveyance for our families a two-horse wagon, which was amply sufficient, there being only fourteen of us all told....When we crossed the ferry we found a gay crowd of probably 300....They were boating in the river, roaming about aimlessly, fishing, courting, listening to the band play, playing in the branch, and waiting for dinner. And ere long the baskets were taken...and the hungry crowd began to play havoc with their contents....Andersonville is the most attractive place we have seen for a picnic in dry weather, but on this occasion there was rather much wetness and it cast a damper upon the*

spirits of the crowd, as it was simply impossible for them to wander over the hills and valleys, gather the flowers wild, and obtain a fair view of the picturesque spot in its entirety, and our people will never be satisfied until they try it over again on some more auspicious day. It was a pity, too, when we think of the pains and expense the good people of Andersonville had put themselves to in arranging for the picnic. Under the superintendence of Miss Fannie Earle, a noble Christian lady, they had cleared off the undergrowth on the island, placed beautiful rustic seats made of birch under the shade trees, built a bridge to the mainland, and arranged everything for the comfort and pleasure of the visitors.

Andersonville hung on until 1893 with a post office and one church, Andersonville Baptist Church, serving the few remaining families who lived there. By the mid-1940s, the land was abandoned, a ghost town on the river. The only remaining residents were the ones buried there. Even Andersonville Baptist Church moved farther inland.

In the 1950s, work began on Hartwell Lake. In May 1950, the federal government passed the Flood Control Act, which authorized the building of Hartwell Dam and Reservoir as part of the development of the Savannah River basin. Construction on the project started in 1955 and was completed in 1963, with the dam being finished in 1959.

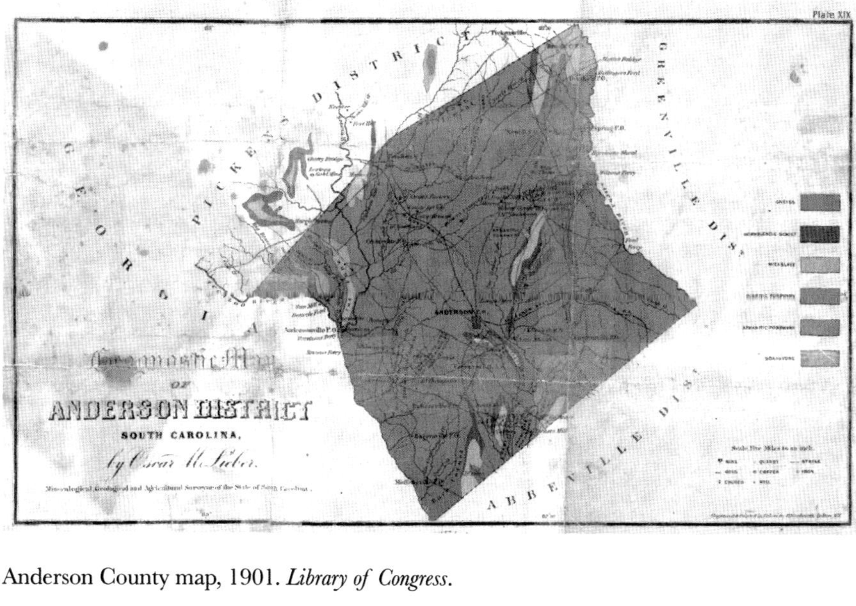

Anderson County map, 1901. *Library of Congress.*

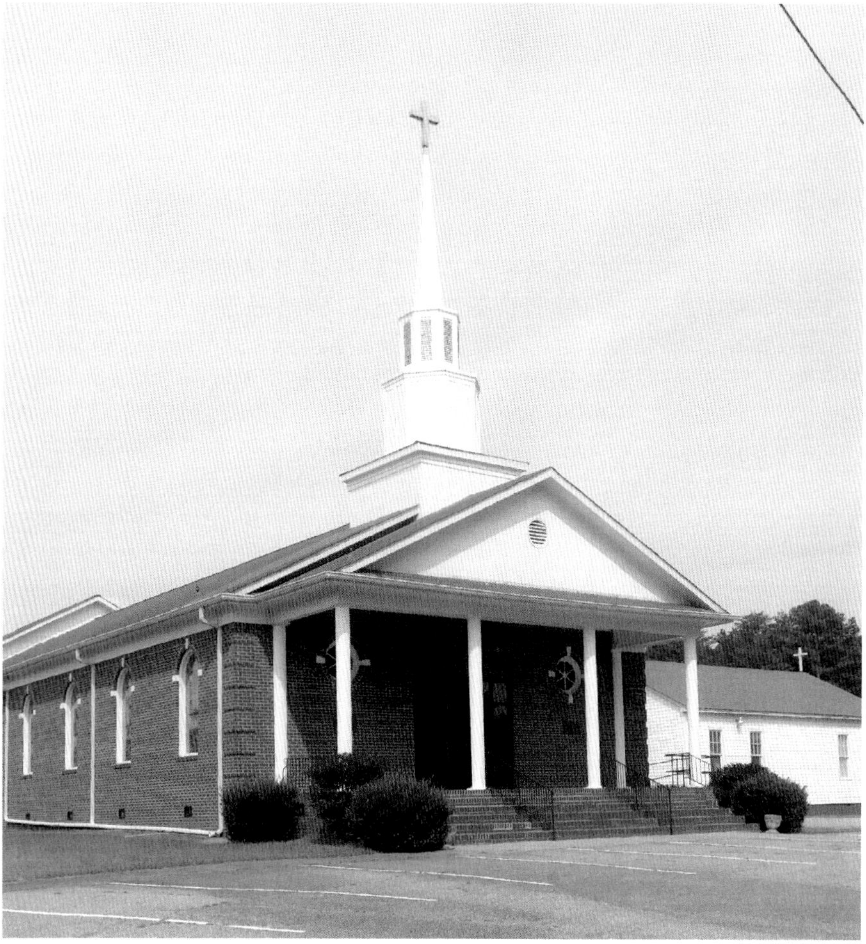

Andersonville Baptist Church in its present location. *Author's collection.*

Of course, the building of the dam meant flooding the valleys below it. The lake created by the dams became Hartwell Lake, which covered all but about four hundred acres of land, turning it into an island. The buried residents in the cemetery of the island were moved to the newly relocated Andersonville Baptist Church.

By the 1960s, the only thing left of the town was falling buildings and tree-covered trails. Adventuring kayakers can still get to the island, and several have blogged about their trips there. It is still a popular destination for partiers and other water travelers.

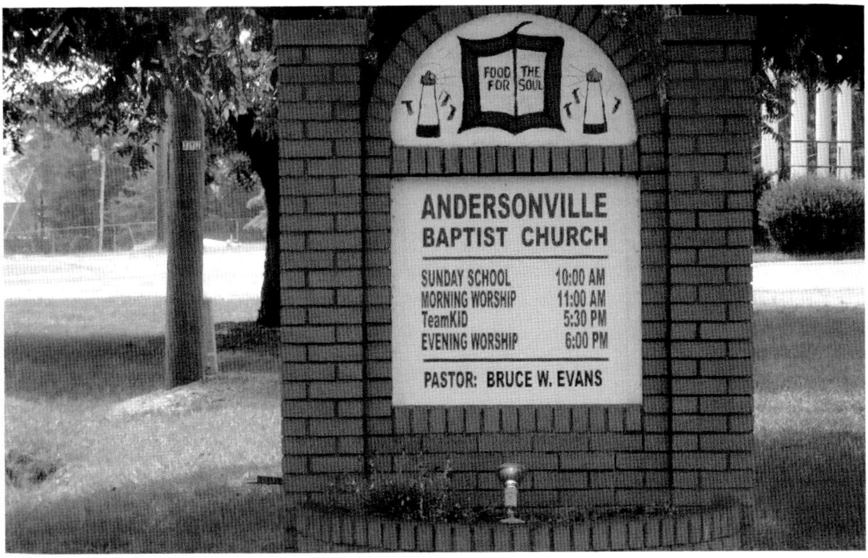

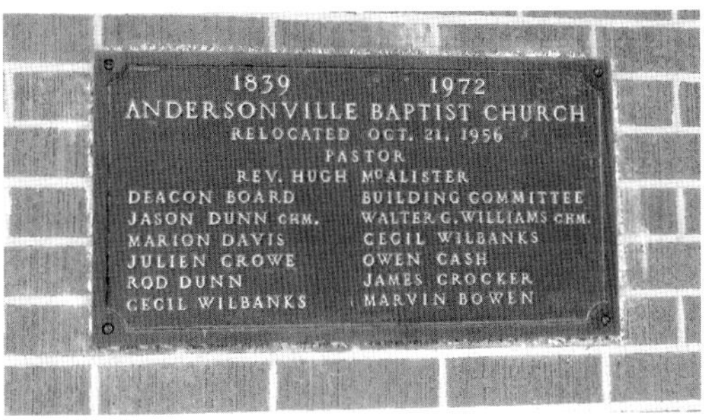

Above: Andersonville Baptist Church on Dobbins Bridge Road was moved to its current location in 1956. *Author's collection.*

Left: The dedication plaque at Andersonville Baptist Church. *Author's collection.*

In 2011, a forest fire, sparked by a fire left unattended by campers, burned more than twenty acres of the island. Owned then by the U.S. Army Corps of Engineers, the island was a powder box of flammable material due to the dead foliage and fallen trees. Firefighters had to contain the blaze to prevent smoke from the fire causing a shutdown on I-85 or posing a health threat to residents in the surrounding areas.

Firefighters were called to the blaze at 4:00 p.m. and had to dig a trench by hand to contain the fire, since they couldn't bring bulldozers to the island to help with the digging. The fire was contained within two hours and continued to burn until it extinguished itself.

5

The Founding of Williamston, a Dream Come True

It was a fall day in 1842, and West Allen Williams was traveling across his property, planning in his head how he would lay out his plantation. For just a little while, he stopped to take a nap under one of the trees that populated the thousands of acres north of Anderson and south of Greenville that he owned.

While he slept, he dreamed. He saw a clear, tumbling spring that healed those who came to it. He saw the sick and the weak come to the spring to sip, and he watched them leave healed. Surely, he thought when he woke, it was a sign. Listening intently, he heard the trickling and gurgling of a spring coming from somewhere on his property. Once he found the source, he knew he would have a mineral spring capable of healing those who came to it.

At least, that's one story of how Mineral Springs in Williamston was found. According to another, a woodcutter named Zahra Kelly knew about the spring and had drunk from it often. He pointed out the spring and its healing powers to Williams. It was Kelly, some said, who had found the spring and proven its healing power.

Regardless, the spring was assumed to bring about good health. It wasn't long before word of Williams's mineral spring spread and the town of Mineral Springs sprang up around it. Within a few years, it became a major resort area, with people from all over the country coming in by railroad to take advantage of the healing power of the town's water.

They called it the "Saratoga of the South," a reference to Saratoga Springs in Upstate New York, to which people also thronged for its healing powers.

At first, people came from all over, pitching tents in the woods around the mineral spring. Then huts and cottages sprang up. Three men from Abbeville finally bought the property surrounding the spring and put up a hotel in the 1850s. It was called the Mammoth Hotel, both for its size and for the money spent on it. The investors are thought to have spent more than $100,000 (the equivalent of $3.125 million today) to erect what was at the time the largest building in South Carolina. It boasted state-of-the-art equipment and amenities for its day, including natural gas fixtures, a bowling alley and 150 rooms. Rooms, it was said, were reportedly always booked.

For years, the hotel and the tourist trade around the spring flourished. But in 1860, the hotel burned to the ground, ending much of the overnight accommodations tourists had come to expect.

Another investor rebuilt the hotel using the same brick and pillars of the old building and putting it on the same site. But this hotel was smaller than the original.

When the Civil War started, the age of mineral springs and tourism in the South faded. Health spas ceased to be popular as brother fought against brother, and with no men to travel with them to the spa, women stopped going as well.

But Williams was undaunted. He laid out plans for his town and worked to make it grow. Two lots were designated as spots for schools, one for boys and one for girls. The boys' high school grew and prospered, but the girls' school withered on the vine. In 1871, though, Dr. Samuel Lander, a Methodist clergyman, opened a school for girls called the Williamston Female College. The school thrived for twenty-six years as a private institution. Lander eventually moved his school to Greenwood and changed its name to Lander College. Since then, the school has grown into a respected four-year coeducational public college, Lander University.

In 1852, when the town changed its name from Mineral Springs to Williamston, Williams deeded the spring and the area around it to the town. His three sons-in-law offered him $5,000 for the land. But Williams refused to sell it. He said that he intended for the mineral spring to be a benefit for the public forever.

From the 1870s through the 1930s, Chautauquas were a cultural movement in America. John Hely Vincent and Lewis Miller started the original Chautauqua Institute in western New York State in 1874. The two men rented an area used for Methodist camp meetings and started a summer school for Sunday school teachers. The intent was educational, not ecumenical. Never affiliated with any one religion or denomination,

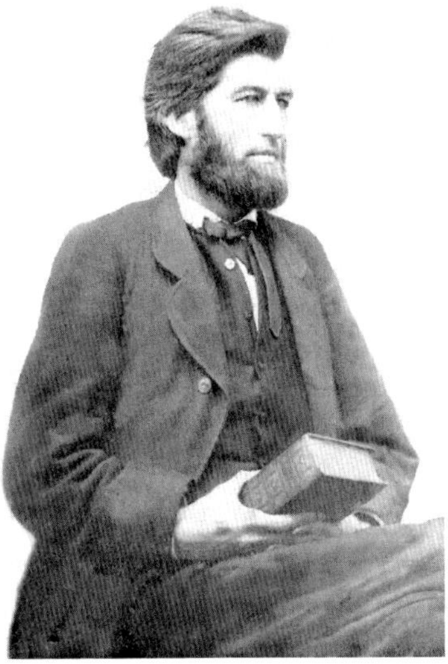

Samuel Lander. *Courtesy of the* Williamston Journal.

the institute grew to encompass all kinds of adult education and incorporated a correspondence course to bring "a college outlook" to the common American. By the 1890s, the Chautauqua Institute was regarded as a school for liberal arts at its most essential.

At the turn of the century, the movement grew, and upwards of 1,200 Chautauquas sprang up across the country. The area around the mineral spring in Williamston became Chautauqua Park and was an area for concerts, lectures and other entertainment for a while. Two hotels, the Bonfire and Park View, were built to accommodate the guests who came from all over to enjoy the programs.

But the spring wasn't always the site of good things. For Edith Dessie Hand, the spring across the street was the witness to great bravery and horrible loss.

Edith and her family, four sisters, two brothers and her parents, lived in Williamston on Main Street, just across from the mineral spring. On August 25, 1915, around 1:30 a.m., the family was asleep when Edith smelled smoke. She screamed for her father. When J.M. Hand, her father, awoke, he found that the entire entryway hall was ablaze. There was no way to get upstairs to the children. Rushing to his wife's room, he roused her and their youngest son, J.M. Jr., and the three escaped through the back door.

Edith called out to her father from the second-floor window. She had two of her younger sisters, Grace, age ten, and Edna Mae, age eight, on the roof of the porch with her. She was urging them to jump. Mr. Hand rushed to them and caught each one as they fell.

Edith then ran back into the burning building to get her six-year-old sister. After she had urged her sister to jump into her father's arms, Edith yelled down to her family, "I'm going back to get brother!"

Roy Hand, her brother, was sleeping in a room across the hall from the girls' room. Edith disappeared into the room. When she opened the door, a wave of fire rushed in, separating her from her brother. The flames burned her neck and chest. She ran out the window and into her father's arms.

With the girls secured, Hand's wife remembered that their youngest, Reba, just thirteen months old, was in her husband's room. Mr. and Mrs. Hand rushed back into the burning building to grab the infant. With the building falling down around them, they were able to rescue the child and get out of the building alive.

A bucket brigade was started, focusing on the west side of the house, where Roy's bedroom had been. Already the building had fallen in over the boy's room. At 3:00 a.m., firefighters were able to retrieve the charred remains from the room. The boy's body was burned to the bones except on the right side. It was assumed that he had been asleep when the fire started and was overcome by smoke and never woke. His remains were wrapped in a sheet and taken to the First Baptist Church for funeral services. He was buried in the Williamston Cemetery.

The family lost everything in the blaze. They were renting the house, so they didn't have insurance on the building. All of their furniture was destroyed. In addition, Hand ran a store in Williamston and was accustomed to taking his accounts home with him each night. He estimated that he lost several hundred dollars in cash that night.

The Hands' home and two other buildings burned that night. The other buildings were owned by J.A. Wallace of Hendersonville, North Carolina. One was a home owned by him, the other an eleven-room hotel, leased from him. Wallace and his family were staying in the home at the time; all of them escaped. No other deaths were reported, but the loss of the buildings was estimated at $7,000, or about $164,000 in today's terms.

Williams died in October 1857 after a brief illness. In his obituary, he was remembered for his public spirit and patriotism. But he wasn't buried in Williamston. Instead, he was interred in an area near Pelzer, close to the graves of his mother and father, Mary and Samuel Williams, and his brother, Samuel Williams Jr. In 2002, Williamston police officer Holly Henderson and her family were four-wheeling in the area and found the family's gravesite, a sealed marble vault.

Williams's body was exhumed. Still intact with some of the clothing with which he was buried remaining, his body, along with those of his family members, were moved to a new resting place inside Mineral Springs Park as part of the town's sesquicentennial.

The town reassembled the graves and the mausoleum as closely as possible to the way they were originally found and placed them near the park. "We are going to give West Allen Williams as much honor as our town can give to him and his family," said Philip Clardy, Williamston's mayor at the time. "You always think he had a vision for the town and you wonder if what it has become is what he hoped for or even more so."

Part II

THE CIVIL WAR AND RECONSTRUCTION

6
Brown's Raiders and Clayton's Store

At the end of the Civil War, Union forces were on the warpath, trying to catch up with Confederate gold.

In addition to being the rumored site of the Confederate treasury, Anderson lay directly in the Union soldiers' path—between the last known location of the gold, Richmond, Virginia, and Abbeville, the birthplace of the Confederacy and supposed location of Confederate president Jefferson Davis. So, it was no surprise that Union troops stormed into town, raiding local stores and looting.

The date was May 1, 1865. The war was all but over. Lee had surrendered to Grant at Appomattox less than a month before, though it would be another month before the last Confederate army, commanded by General Edmund Kirby Smith, surrendered to Union negotiators, bringing a formal end to the bloodiest four years in U.S. history.

Elsewhere in South Carolina, people were moving on, some even honoring the dead. In Charleston, former slaves, now free, honored the Union dead by digging up the bodies of more than 250 Union soldiers to give them a proper burial. For more than two weeks, the newly freed slaves worked to show their gratitude to the men who had died fighting for their emancipation. When they were done, the slaves held a parade led by black children to memorialize the dead.

Some say this was the beginning of Memorial Day in the United States. But it wasn't until 1868 that Major General John A. Logan, head of the Grand Army of the Republic, established Decoration Day as a time for the country to honor the dead, both Union and Confederate. Flowers were placed on these Civil War graves for the first time on May 30 of that year.

The first large observance of Decoration Day was held in Arlington National Cemetery, the former home of General Robert E. Lee. The veranda of the house was shrouded in mourning drapes, and various Washington officials, including General and Mrs. Ulysses S. Grant, presided over the ceremonies. After speeches and other observances, children from the Soldiers' and Sailors' Orphan Home and members of the Grand Army of the Republic (GAR) walked through the cemetery, laying flowers on the graves of Union and Confederate soldiers. It's widely considered the first Memorial Day.

In 1865 in Anderson, hidden in the basements of many stores were the valuables of South Carolina refugees from Charleston and Columbia. In fact, many of the Lowcountry refugees themselves were hiding throughout the area. When Union general William Tecumseh Sherman offered up Savannah to Lincoln on Christmas Day in 1864, Charlestonians naturally assumed their town was next. Many fled inland to their summer homes. When Sherman turned to Columbia instead, one of the sub-treasuries of the Confederacy was moved to University Hill in Anderson to avoid capture.

Andersonians, however, took that in stride. Secure in the thought that their out-of-the-way town was safe, residents ignored talk of coming Union soldiers. When the bright May Day sun shone over the Piedmont hills, the folks of Anderson felt safely tucked away from the last days of the Civil War.

Then word reached town that cadets from The Citadel had clashed with raiders near Williamston. Anderson residents still weren't concerned, though, as many assumed that the Union raiders would move on across the Saluda River to Greenville.

At the time, though, the Confederacy was scrambling. Rumor had it that when Richmond fell, fleeing Rebel soldiers smuggled the Confederate treasury—said by some accounts to include gold and jewelry worth $100,000 and, by others, into the millions—into train cars and onto horseback to rush the assets to Abbeville, where Davis was said to be hiding.

It was because of Anderson's out-of-the-way location that it was considered to be a natural hiding place. That kind of thinking made Anderson a Union target.

General George Thomas had ordered scattered brigades commanded by General George Stoneman, otherwise known as the infamous leader of Stoneman's Raiders, to go on the march. Thomas suggested the brigades meet up in Anderson. Thus, the cavalry came at Anderson from

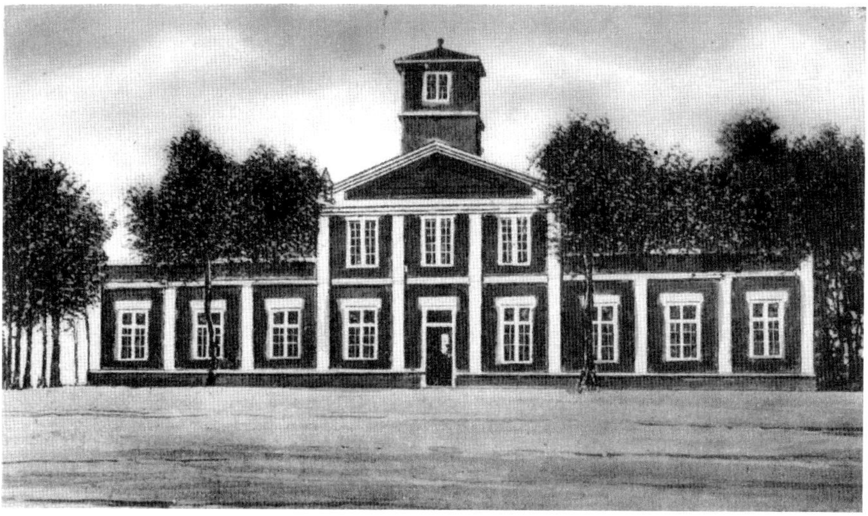

Confederate Treasury, circa 1900. *Courtesy of South Caroliniana Library, University of South Carolina, Columbia, South Carolina.*

different directions, resulting in skirmishes near Pendleton, Williamston and Craytonville.

Also en route to Anderson were cadets from the Arsenal Academy in Columbia. Like a prep school for The Citadel, Arsenal Academy trained its students for combat, and indeed they were ready for battle. The cadets had fled Columbia before Sherman invaded in February. They spent the next month on marches through western North Carolina and Upstate South Carolina before making camp in Greenville.

Reports had been coming in for weeks that Stoneman and his raiders were on their way through Tennessee and Georgia, headed to the Upstate in an effort to bring the same destruction to South Carolina that Sherman had wrought from Savannah to Columbia.

Presumably, Stoneman's first goal was to capture Greenville and send his raiders along the Greenville and Columbia Railroad to lay waste to everything in their path. Instead, around April 29 or 30, they came upon the Arsenal cadets and fired on them. Hoping to avoid a fight, the cadets retreated to Greenville. Once there, the group was given orders to return to Columbia. At midnight, the cadets set off, stopping shortly for a break near Shiloh Methodist Church near Williamston.

On the morning of May 1, Stoneman's Raiders stumbled across them again. For only a few moments, the two groups fired at each other. James

Spearman of Newberry was shot in the hand. A Union soldier was shot off his horse and wounded badly. His company left him to die.

Local women who witnessed the shooting of the Union soldier begged the cadets not to kill him. The cadets agreed and took the man to a hospital in Greenville, where he was nursed back to health. He later married one of the women who rescued him.

This skirmish came to be called the Battle of Anderson. It is recreated every year by reenactors in open fields near Williamston.

Meanwhile, the Union troops headed on to Anderson. Leading the raid was General Simeon Brown, of St. Clair, Michigan. The proprietor of an inn before the war, the fifty-three-year-old man had been appointed to the rank of major by the governor of Michigan and had risen to general in less than three years. Brown was an interim commander who oversaw more than 1,900 cavalrymen from Tennessee, Kentucky and Michigan. His men had a reputation for looting and undisciplined behavior, practices he did little to prevent.

For three days in 1865, from May 1 to 3, Brown's Raiders and others menaced the town, according to the *Anderson Intelligencer*. Anderson resident Judge J.P. Reed understood that the war was already lost and intended to convince Andersonians to give up rather than fight.

"We would have been destroyed," his daughter Emmala Reed wrote in her journal. "We heard they hoped some defense would have been made here, for this was the hotbed of Secession and they wished to ruin us."

The Yankee troops entered Anderson with little advance warning. Word of the march traveled slower than the brigades, and besides, people had been talking about impending raids for months, but few if any had done anything about it. No one was prepared or worried about their arrival. Andersonians had resolved to go on with life as usual.

According to some accounts, the Union troops came into town riding horses and firing their weapons. The Union troops had heard the rumor that the Confederate gold and silver were hidden away in Anderson and went through the town looking for it. They ransacked homes looking for the treasury and tortured residents for clues as to where the Confederate treasure was stashed away.

In fact, the previous February, when Sherman's troops had marched toward Columbia, the treasury's printing presses and plates had been moved to the Johnson Female Seminary on Anderson's South Main Street. The school had been closed because of the war, and the empty building in the remote town served as a perfect spot to hide the secessionist

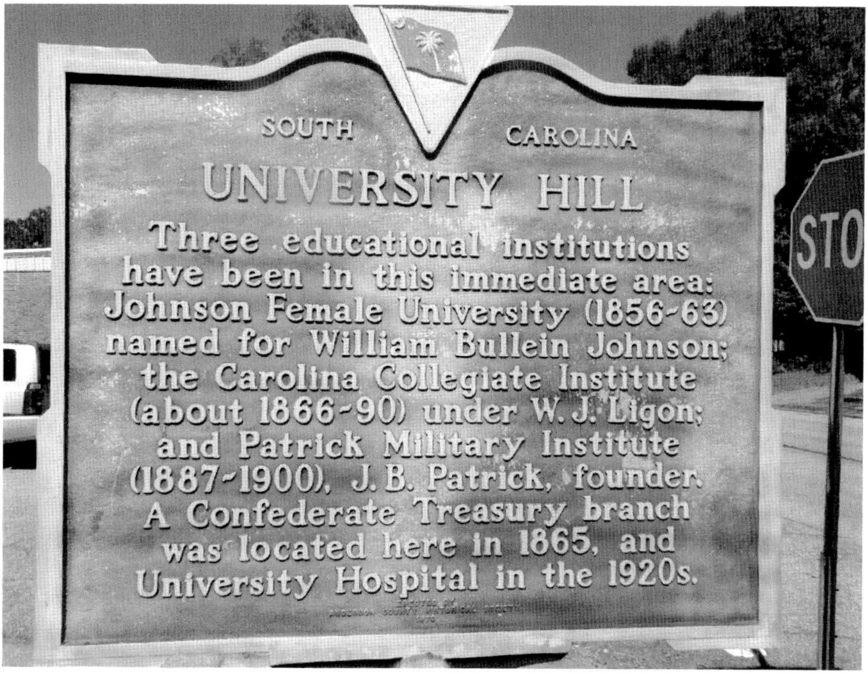

Confederate Treasury marker on South Main Street, Anderson. *Author's collection.*

government's currency-printing machine and treasury. But without gold or silver to back the money, it was essentially worthless. Nevertheless, the Confederacy continued to print "graybacks" to pay for the war.

Raiders found the treasury building and entered it, breaking up the presses, smashing the plates and throwing the paper intended for the presses into the street. Because of the scarcity of paper, residents rushed into the street to gather up the bits. Emmala Reed wrote in her journal:

> *The wild crew tore up everything in the depot—cars & railroad—fruit &c. Then on to the University—the Treasury Dp't now, which no doubt attracted them here. We could hear the destruction all morning, as all the iron presses & works were broken to pieces & confederate paper money scattered all over the earth—books &c burned up. All totally demolished! Much of the money was not signed and valueless. So it all will be soon. Every negro & child had piles of it. Hundreds of dollars which we took as worthless, but 'tis so useless and so humiliating now to think that this is the fate of our currency and our Gov't!*

> *Mr. Myers, who suffered so much in Columbia, had spasms since, and was hung up until nearly dead, to make him reveal about their gold—failed. Dr. Cater's place and clothes torn up. He hung up for the same purpose. So at the Winthrops: Dr. W was hung up & beaten with a shovel. Even good old Mrs. W threatened with hanging. The Ruccors' house, being empty, was sacked—furniture and & destroyed. Whitner's house threatened with burning, Mrs. Glover & other ladies made to play the piano for them.*
>
> *Elias Earle's family suffered most perhaps—pointed out as rich. Palmer's brigade—coming from Greenville—had camped there. He & staff in the house, but protected nothing. Destroyed all the provisions & clothes. Took negroes & made them give up jewels and silver & gold. Shot at the ladies & made them produce the buried treasure or would burn. Started to hang up poor Preston, but all stood out bravely. Said burn or hang, I won't yield.*
>
> *On the whole, no lives were lost, & everyone can manage to live, I guess. Many horses were taken, but they left mean ones behind and gave to other people. So some crops can be made, perhaps. A fearful prospect still, but thank heavens it was no worse.*

Out of concern for others' safety, Judge Reed hatched a plan: Get the Yankees drunk and hope they leave town and let Anderson escape unscathed.

Knowing that Brown's men meant to ride the thirty miles east to Abbeville in an effort to catch President Davis, Reed told Brown about a different "treasure" hidden under B.F. Crayton's Store. Located on the courthouse square, Crayton's Store held a fortune worth of alcohol in the form of wines and liquor from overseas. Hundreds of bottles of wines like Madeira and port had been shipped to the last stop on the rail line from Charleston when Sherman burned Savannah.

On the coast, Charlestonians, fearing for their lives and fortunes and certain that Sherman's next stop was their city, had headed northwest. Charleston wine merchant Henry Guardine decided to move his wares to where his customers were going.

Dr. Reed told Brown about the wine cellar late in the afternoon. His goal was to save the town, pacifying the nearly two thousand raiders with alcohol until they got orders to move.

His daughter wasn't so sure the plan would work. Emmala wrote in her journal: "Pa pointed out to him a building where were stored quantities of liquors of Mr. Guardine of Charleston—wine merchant. At least $200,000 worth of splendid old wines—brandies &c considered invaluable by these men, but ought to have been destroyed—to prevent drunkenness and ruin here which was visited upon Columbia. He [General Brown] promised to keep his soldiers from it, but didn't try. They were soon breaking in and drinking madly, and all trembled for the effects."

It was a risky move. Brown's troops weren't known for being a well-mannered, well-disciplined and easygoing bunch. The company was thought by many to be out of control. General William Palmer would later send a report to Stoneman about Brown's troops, saying: "Their officers for the most part have lost all control over their men. A large number of the men and some of the officers devote themselves exclusively to pillaging and destroying property. General Brown appears to have given them carte blanche in South Carolina, and they are now so entirely destitute of discipline that it cannot be restored in the field."

The troops drank their fill and continued their pillaging and marauding of the town until they finally passed out. What could have been a massive blow to the town was a minor one instead. But it wasn't the end.

On May 2, Brown's troops slid out of town early. Word reached the company that Stoneman's Raiders were on their way, and the troops immediately left to avoid being found by the larger, more regimented force.

First, however, two thousand Union cavalry troops under the command of General William Palmer entered town in the dead of night under a flag of truce. Palmer was after Jefferson Davis, and his men were ordered to rest a while in Anderson. They did so—until they found the wine, that is.

Men drank canteens full of wine and poured barrels of it out into the streets. For two days, Union troops came to Anderson intent on finding Confederate gold and traces of Jefferson Davis, but they stayed and strayed from their mission because of the wine. With no Andersonians killed and no Anderson buildings burned to the ground, some say Reed's plan was a success. Still others say the looting of Anderson and the torture of some of its residents meant that Reed's plan to distract Union forces wasn't completely successful.

One thing remains certain, though: Union forces that entered Anderson didn't follow after Davis. As the soldiers settled in for a good time, Davis was able to hold the last war council for the Confederacy before escaping the raiders one last time.

On May 3, the last day of the siege of Anderson, a third outfit arrived. Likely associated with Kirk's Raiders under Colonel George Kirk, they were responsible for the only fatality over the three days of raids.

By then, only a few Union soldiers remained in town. Emmala Reed wrote in her journal that several members of the provost guard (a self-appointed police force) came to her father looking for arms to go out and arrest straggling Union troops. Reed advised against it. He didn't want the men to upset the soldiers at all. His plan to lay low and wait it out had worked so far, he said, and he felt the town could get away without any more damage or bloodshed.

But one member of the provost guard, seventeen-year-old McKenzie Parker, a cadet at the Arsenal Academy in Columbia who had been caught up in the Battle of Anderson days earlier, stayed in Anderson to defend his home. Reed begged the provost guard not to cause trouble. Ignoring him, Parker and his friends set out to confront the Yankees. When Kirk's Raiders began to show up, the provost guard took their places. Union soldiers rode up East Benson Street to South Main. Parker and his friends were in the courthouse square, near Crayton's Store.

Threats and gunshots were exchanged. Parker ordered the soldiers to halt, but they refused. He raised his gun and pulled the trigger. But the gun misfired. A Union soldier shot back, hitting Parker in the chest. His friends carried him into a nearby hotel, where he died shortly after.

Parker would have been a member of The Citadel's class of 1868. Because the school closed from 1865 until 1882, he was unable to go to the Charleston military academy as planned. Still, The Citadel lists Parker as one of its "fallen alumni" and notes him as the "last Confederate death."

Years later, in 1902, a statue honoring "Our Confederate Dead," topped by a granite Confederate private at parade rest, was erected near the spot where Parker died. The Confederate private has stood watch over downtown Anderson ever since.

In the years since the end of the Civil War, rumors of the treasure of Confederate gold have persisted. Some say it never made it to South Carolina at all and was buried in Wilkes County, North Carolina, where Davis was said to have stayed. Others say it is in Washington, Georgia, where Davis was captured. Even more say there was never a treasure at all.

What is known is that on April 2, 1865, after church services, Davis heard of the breakdown of Lee's defensive line at Petersburg, Virginia. Davis pleaded with Lee for one more day as he told his cabinet members to evacuate Richmond and take the Confederate treasury with them.

Lee told Davis he had until 8:00 p.m. Davis loaded gold, valuables and his cabinet members onto two trains on the only rail line open between Richmond and Danville, Virginia. The two trains left at midnight—one

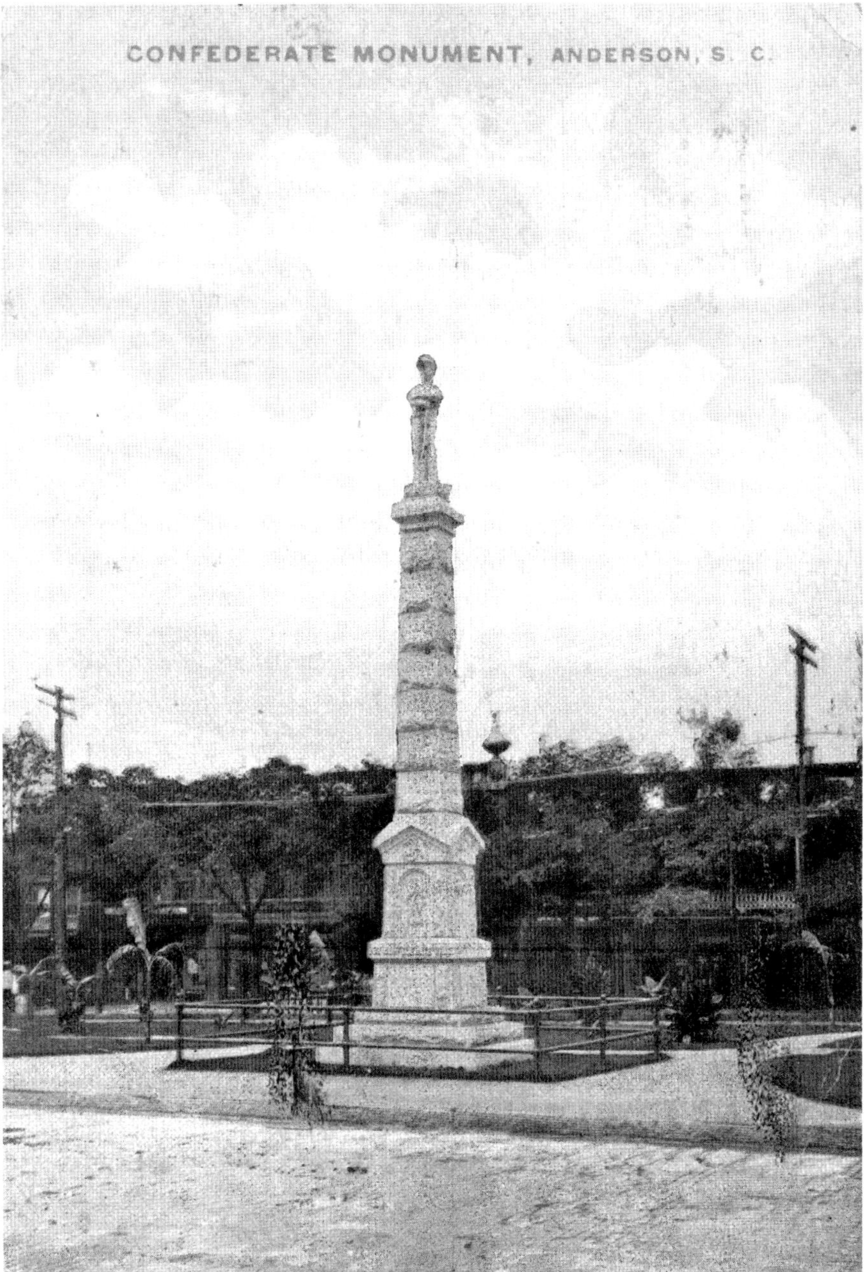

Confederate monument, circa 1910. *Courtesy of South Caroliniana Library, University of South Carolina, Columbia, South Carolina.*

carrying the Confederacy's cabinet members and the other carrying the Confederate treasury. At the end of the line, Davis and his cabinet took off southbound on horseback. The treasury moved first toward the U.S. Mint in Charlotte, until it was discovered that the U.S. Calvary was already in place there.

To elude robbers and Union forces, the treasury was then transferred into smaller containers—kitchen and ammunition containers—to hide what was inside. The wagons took off south, zigzagging their way multiple times across the South Carolina–Georgia state line as they made their way to Washington, Georgia. It is there, at Chennault Plantation, where many believe the treasure is buried, because it was there that Davis and his staff were captured along with a portion of the treasury.

In November 1945, a Colonel Robert Welborn Pickens told the *Anderson Daily Mail* that he had seen the treasury. Colonel Pickens, one of the last living Confederate soldiers, told the paper that he had seen kegs of the gold from the treasury on a railcar traveling through Anderson.

Pickens was a member of Company G in the Second Battalion of the State Reserve of South Carolina in 1865. According to the article, Pickens said Confederate guards had moved a gold-laden train car to a railroad in Anderson. At a stop on the old Greenville and Columbia Railroad, Pickens was on guard the night the train came through, and he saw the kegs of gold as the train stopped in Anderson.

Pickens died at the age of one hundred a short time after the article ran.

The Confederate gold has never officially been found.

7
The Trial of the Nineteenth Century

Life after the Civil War was tough.

As part of Reconstruction, once-prosperous farm owners found themselves with destroyed property and no way to farm it—and no way to pay the taxes on it. Many sold their lands to Northern carpetbaggers just to survive.

Additionally, martial law had been declared in the Southern states to control the former Confederates and help ease the transition to a society where blacks were freedmen.

It was under martial law that the "Trial of the Nineteenth Century" in Anderson County began. As part of martial law, the occupying forces of the Union army, specifically the First Battalion Maine Infantry commanded by twenty-eight-year-old Lieutenant Colonel Calvin S. Brown, were in charge of Anderson Courthouse, as Anderson was then known.

Crawford Keys, a local landholder, lived two miles west of Anderson and owned cotton that he wished to have shipped to Augusta. Keys, a farmer and a railroad builder, had worked during part of the war as an agent of the Quartermaster Department for the Confederacy. He was also a member of the Provost Court, a military tribunal for minor offenses.

Gaines Stowers, a farmer and transporter, lived in Georgia about a mile west of Brown's Ferry. He had been Hart County sheriff and served two terms in the Georgia Senate. Stowers agreed to ship the cotton for Keys. The cotton was shipped to Brown's Ferry on the left bank of the Savannah River.

On October 2, 1865, two U.S. Treasury agents ordered William Brown, the owner of the ferry, to hold the cotton. Two days later, William Brown told Keys, his son Robert and Stowers what he'd been ordered to do. Keys was not pleased and, accordingly, asked Brown to move the cotton anyway. Brown refused and let Lieutenant Colonel Brown know what Keys wanted. In response, Brown stationed three soldiers at the ferry to guard the cotton.

On October 8, witnesses reported that a group of men had come to the ferry and that "scuffling, voices and shots were heard." The next morning, the bodies of the three soldiers—Corporal William Corbett, twenty-two, of Eastport, Maine, and Privates Emery Smith, nineteen, of Hallowell, Maine, and Mason Brown, twenty, of Lubec, Maine—were found in the river. The medical examiner reported that Corbett and Brown had both been shot in the temple with a pistol that had been held to their heads. Smith had been shot through the jaw from cheek to cheek. He didn't die from his gunshots but from drowning, the examiner said.

Immediately, Lieutenant Colonel Brown suspected Keys. Brown arrested him and his son Robert on October 11. Brown also arrested Stowers and Elisha Byrum, a farmer and neighbor of Keys. The officer charged the men with murder.

Andersonians were concerned. Many couldn't believe that Keys and Stowers could have murdered the three young men, but others were worried any public outcry would make things more difficult for them during the military occupation.

On October 13, several members of the Anderson Courthouse community met to discuss the situation. Under the guidance of Colonel James Lawrence Orr, who was running for governor at the time, the citizens condemned the actions and pledged their full cooperation with the military in their investigation of the crime. They also sent their sympathy to the families of the fallen Union servicemen.

At first, the accused were sent to a jail in Columbia to await trial. But in November, Major General Daniel E. Sickles took over the command of the Department of South Carolina. Sickles, who operated by the book, saw the crime as particularly heinous and vicious and ordered the accused men moved to Charleston. Soon after, they were transferred to Fort Pinckney in Charleston, a damp jail located one mile off the coast in the harbor. Testimony in the trial states that the prisoners were held "with manacles upon their wrists and [shackles] upon their ankles…guarded by vicious and ribald Negro troops."

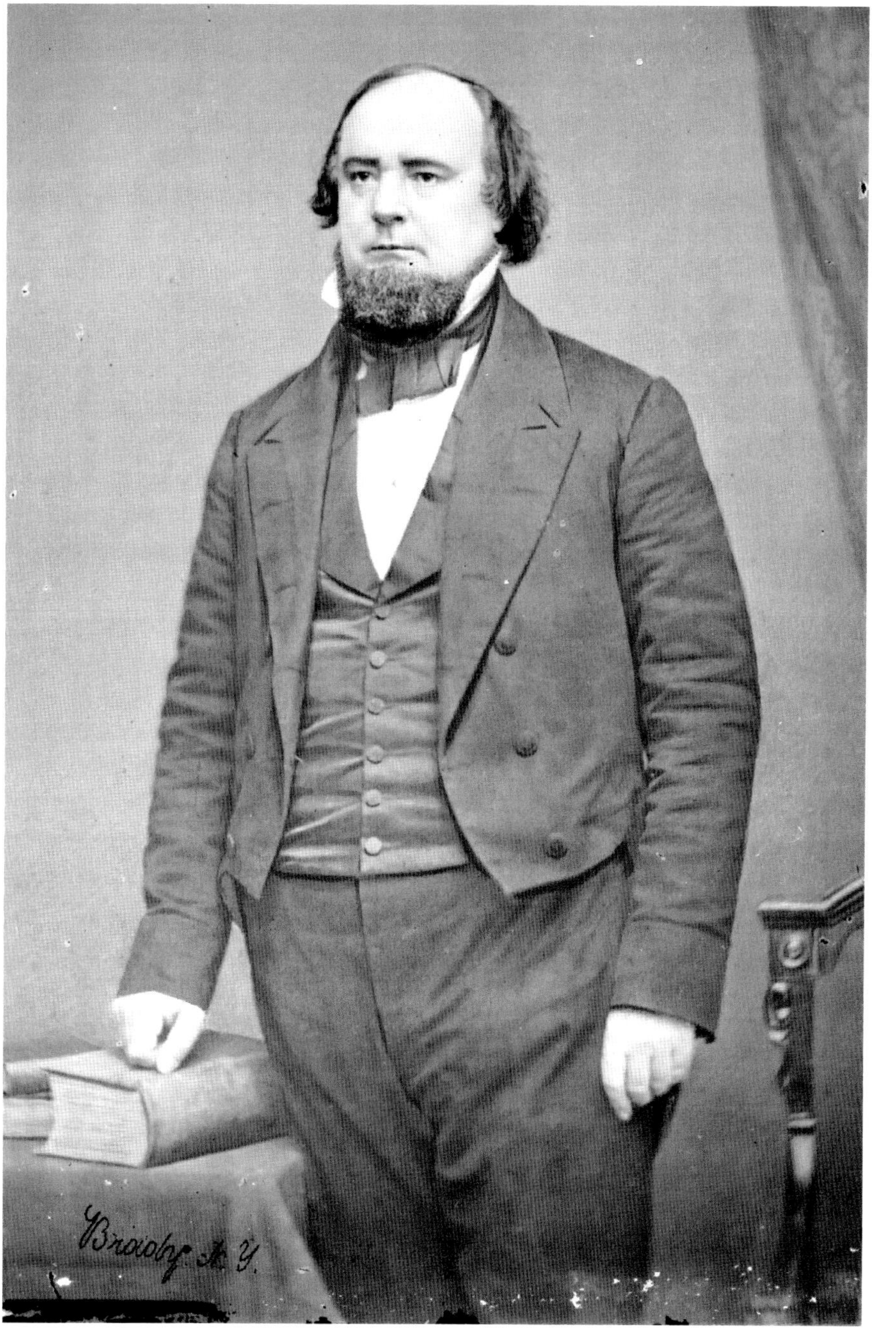

James Lawrence Orr. *Library of Congress.*

Although the group asked Orr to be their lawyer, Orr turned them down, worried that it could color the pending election and that the trial would interfere with his inauguration should he win. Instead, Armistad Burt, sixty-two, of Abbeville agreed to represent them.

Earlier in the year, Sickles's predecessor had issued General Order No. 102, which proclaimed that "Offenses by citizens requiring a severe punishment, will be tried by a military commission." However, a conflict of the courts arose. As a compromise, another general order was issued: "Provost courts...shall have...exclusive cognizance to try and adjudicate all cases wherein freedmen and other persons of color are concerned." All other cases were supposed to be tried by civil courts and in accordance with the laws of South Carolina in force immediately before November 17, 1860.

On January 2, Keys and his group were brought to trial by military commission at The Citadel.

First, the military commission tried Stowers alone. At the end of the trial, in his summation, Burt protested the proceedings. "I stand in the presence of a Military Court, organized for the administration of martial law....Instead of the scales of justice, I see...the sword....Instead of a hall dedicated to justice, I find...a military camp....This fearful trial, the mandate of the conqueror, is held in a conquered country and a captive city."

Instead of announcing their findings in regard to Stowers, the commission decided to reserve judgment until the conclusion of the trial of all the prisoners.

The trial of Crawford Keys, Robert Keys and Elisha Byrum started on March 3, 1866. Each of the men was charged with attacking a guard, murder, robbery and seditious conspiracy and riot. The sedition charge stemmed from an incident that had occurred on January 1, 1861.

Each of the men pleaded not guilty to the first three charges. As to the charge of sedition, the men argued that the commission had no jurisdiction over any occurrence prior to Lee surrendering to Sherman in April 1865. The commission deliberated over the fourth charge and ultimately dropped it.

On March 5, the prosecution's first witness, William F. Brown, took the stand. Brown testified that on the night of the murders he went to bed at 8:00 p.m. and at about 9:00 p.m. a man calling from the opposite bank of the river awakened him. Brown woke up his ferryman, Warren Howell, who ferried the man across. Brown said he returned to bed. Around 11:00 or 12:00, he said, he "raised up to the window" and saw a group of six or seven men walking on the road past his house, headed to the ferry. Brown swore that it was a clear, still night and that the moon was shining.

"I think I knew two of the men, Crawford Keys and Stowers," he said. Describing Keys as wearing blue cotton pants and a light-colored coat, Brown said he saw Keys's face as he came through the gate. Brown said after the men passed, he went to Howell's house and asked if he had seen the men. Brown then returned to his yard and shortly thereafter "heard a fuss at the river."

"The first thing I heard was an order to 'throw down your arms,'" he testified. "It was Stowers who said that, but Keys who gave the order 'Fall in here, men.'"

"Then there was a cap burst. There was a general fuss then, stamping and cursing around," he testified. "Then I heard some five or six guns fired. Seemed to me there was three or four guns went off together, and directly afterwards two guns within a second or two. I heard someone speak…after the guns were fired and say 'It is time we were gone.'"

Returning to his home from his backyard, Brown said that he saw three men on horses and a glimpse of a man walking behind them. After they passed by his gate, he didn't see them again.

The next day, Howell testified. He recounted the night of October 8 with the same story of a man crossing the river around 8:00 p.m. from the Georgia side. Howell said the man appeared to be keeping his identity a secret and offered Howell a drink. But Howell said he recognized the man as Peter Keys.

Later, he said he was in his yard as a group of men passed by his gate. He told the commission that some of them ordered the soldiers to surrender and that they had "come to put them in the river." Then, he said, he heard a shuffling in the flatboat on the river.

"The guards were shot and throwed into the river," Howell told the court. "Next I seed or heard was three men come out riding, and the next three was walking. One that was riding ordered me to go into the house and stay there. I recognized the man's voice as the same one I'd heard at the river. It was Peter Keys's voice, if I'm not mightily mistaken."

Howell identified the four defendants as the men he saw that night. On cross-examination, Howell admitted that he had given contradictory testimony in Stowers's trial. In that trial, Howell had said the night was dark, that he did not know the man who crossed on the ferry and that he didn't recognize any of the men who had come to where the guards were that night. Howell was arrested and placed into solitary confinement. The next day, he changed his story and swore the story he told at Stowers's trial was false.

The next witness, Frederick Clark, was a black millwright and carpenter whose wife worked at Keys' Spring, the Keys farm. Clark testified that he saw Crawford and Robert Keys ride off about eight o'clock that night and return the next morning.

Several of Keys's former slaves were also called to testify. They said they couldn't be sure whether Crawford Keys was at the house or had left the house on horseback that night.

The defense called Governor Orr to the stand. A former member of the South Carolina House of Representatives and later a senator, Orr was an imposing figure on the stand. He stated that on the morning after the murders, Crawford Keys came to Orr's Anderson Courthouse home and asked him to intervene on Keys's behalf regarding Lieutenant Colonel Brown's orders so that Keys could get his cotton back, some of which had been paid to him by the Confederate government. With their business ended, Orr said, he and Keys rode into town and found a crowd at the army's headquarters. When the two men inquired as to what had happened, they were told three soldiers who had been guarding Brown's Ferry had been killed.

Orr said that he then asked Keys if he were out that night; Keys told him that he and Robert had been at home.

Other defense witnesses then testified against some of the prosecution witnesses. Elias Earle, a farmer and miller in the town, testified that he had known Warren Howell since boyhood and that he was not a man to be trusted. Earle also said that William Brown had told him the morning after the murder that he did not recognize any of the marauding men.

More men from the community testified to Howell's lack of character and Crawford Keys's abundance of it. "Howell's character is not good for veracity, I could not believe him on his oath," said Andrew O. Norris, a former commissioner of equity in Anderson. "I have known Crawford Keys for almost forty years and the others from almost infancy. Their characters are good."

Several other men testified that a group of men dressed the same as the soldiers had been seen heading in the direction of Brown's Ferry on the night of the murders, or away from Brown's Ferry the next morning.

After several more weeks of testimony, the two sides closed their cases. Meanwhile, in Washington, D.C., on April 2, President Andrew Johnson declared that the insurrection had ended, and he restored habeas corpus. During the war, President Abraham Lincoln had suspended habeas corpus, in effect placing all persons held by military personnel in the care of military tribunals.

In the court system, habeas corpus protects those charged with crimes from the government just locking them up and throwing away the key. When an attorney challenges a client's detention by filing a habeas corpus petition, the executive branch must explain to a neutral judge its justification for holding the person. Habeas corpus is supposed to protect prisoners from being held indefinitely. It has been a pillar of Western law since the signing of the Magna Carta in England in 1215. In fact, it was so important to the founders of the United States that it was written into the first article of the Constitution.

The next day, April 3, Chief Justice Salmon P. Chase declared unconstitutional Lincoln's edict suspending habeas corpus.

But the trial of Keys and the others by military commission at The Citadel continued. As the two sides presented their summations, the defense focused on discrediting the testimonies offered against the defendants and reiterating the testimonials of their clients' good character. The prosecution offered reasons for Howell's and Brown's conflicting testimonies and questioned the honesty of the members of Crawford Keys's family and the former slaves who had offered testimony on his behalf.

Court adjourned for the day while the commission deliberated. The next day, the commission returned with its verdict. All four men were found guilty of all three charges and were sentenced to hang. However, the commission commuted the sentences of Robert Keys and Elisha Byrum, because they were young men operating under the influence of Crawford Keys.

Sickles set the execution date for April 27 at Castle Pinckney for Stowers and Crawford Keys. Robert Keys and Elisha Byrum were to be transferred to the state prison in Concord, New Hampshire.

ANDERSON REACTS

The news that Crawford Keys and Gaines Stowers were sentenced to die reached Anderson, and the rest of the South, on April 22, 1866—just five days before they were to hang.

News reports suggested that the Anderson community, and many other communities in the South, were preparing themselves for a celebration of a verdict of acquittal. Instead, communities were stunned with Keys's sentence, especially for his not having an opportunity to say goodbye to his family.

Charlestonians reached out to the one man who could do something about it—President Andrew Johnson. I.M. Walton of Charleston wrote to the president and implored him to delay the execution order and hand Keys and Stowers over to civil courts, where they should have been tried in the first place. More than 1,500 Charlestonians signed his letter, and 35 citizens signed a similar petition in Walhalla.

On April 23, Johnson ordered Sickles to suspend the execution until further order and to transmit records of the case to Judge Advocate General Joseph Holt so that Holt could review the case and report to the president. Sickles had no choice but to delay the execution.

More letters from Anderson flooded the president's office, offering up character references for Keys and Stowers and proclaiming that the two men couldn't be guilty. Even Governor Orr wrote to Johnson, asking him to commute the sentences so that the true guilty parties could be brought to trial and convicted. More petitions from Anderson and Hart County, Georgia, were sent to the president, as were letters from all over the country.

William Trescot from Pendleton, a lawyer and distinguished essayist and historian, was called before Holt. In a memorandum, he wrote that having the trial of Stowers separate from the others and trying the three others together, but holding all the verdicts until the end, prejudiced the cases against them all. Trescot also pointed out that Howell perjured himself in one of the trials but that it was impossible to tell which, since evidence not allowed in one case was allowed in the other, and vice versa. In the end, he recommended that justice would be "subserved if the whole finding of the Commission were set aside and the accused handed over to the jurisdiction of the county."

But General Holt submitted to the president a report that said the "prisoners were mutually and equally concerned in the perpetration of the monstrous crime alleged, not only barbarous, but contributing, if permitted to go unpunished, a most dangerous assault upon the dignity and supremacy of the national government, fraught with extreme peril to every officer and man of the United States service whose duty it is to enforce the national authority in the section so recently the seat of armed rebellion and open war against the people of the United States."

Representatives from Anderson then rode to Washington and hired the law firm of Browning and Ewing to represent the prisoners before the president.

Browning dealt the case its fatal blow. In his brief to the president, he noted that not only did the evidence not point to the prisoners' guilt, but also that the Supreme Court had found that military tribunals could not take the place of civil court in the cases of offenses against municipal laws committed by persons with no connection to the military. Browning asked the president to set aside the military commission's findings and leave the prisoners to be tried in Anderson's courts.

At this point, Burt (Keys's attorney) petitioned the court for habeas corpus, in essence asking the military to present evidence as to why they were detaining Keys and the men, or to release them. The writ of habeas corpus was delivered to Sickles. His response was that the prisoners were no longer his, but that they were held in military custody by the authority of the president. Saying that he had no authority to release the prisoners without direct orders from President Johnson, Sickles opted not to present the prisoners.

The prisoners' attorneys called on the judge to find Sickles in contempt of court. As first, the judge refused, asking the men to work it out between attorneys. But the district attorney at the time said he didn't represent Sickles and that he couldn't approach him without the president's authority.

Judge Bryan threw up his hands and said he had no alternative but to find Sickles in contempt and order him arrested by July 10.

Keys's and Stowers's attorneys wired the president and asked him to order Sickles to obey the court. But Secretary of War Edwin Stanton sent Sickles a note instead telling him essentially to stay the course. Stanton told Sickles to "neither give up the prisoners nor submit to arrest, but take into custody all persons attempting to arrest you."

July 10 arrived with no Sickles and no prisoners. When word of Sickles's actions reached the president, Johnson described Sickles as a "conceited cuckold." Johnson wrote to Stanton asking why the writ of habeas corpus should not be obeyed. Stanton, instead of responding to the president, ordered Sickles to transfer the prisoners to Fort Jefferson, Dry Tortugas.

Fort Jefferson was one of the largest nineteenth-century forts in America. Located seventy miles west of Key West on Garden Key, the fort is only accessible by boat. It was designed to protect the harbor off the end of Florida and was a vital part of the Union's campaign to blockade Southern shipping. During the Civil War, the fort was also used as a prison, mainly for Union deserters. Its most famous prisoner was Dr. Samuel Mudd, the doctor who reset John Wilkes Booth's broken leg after his assassination of President Lincoln.

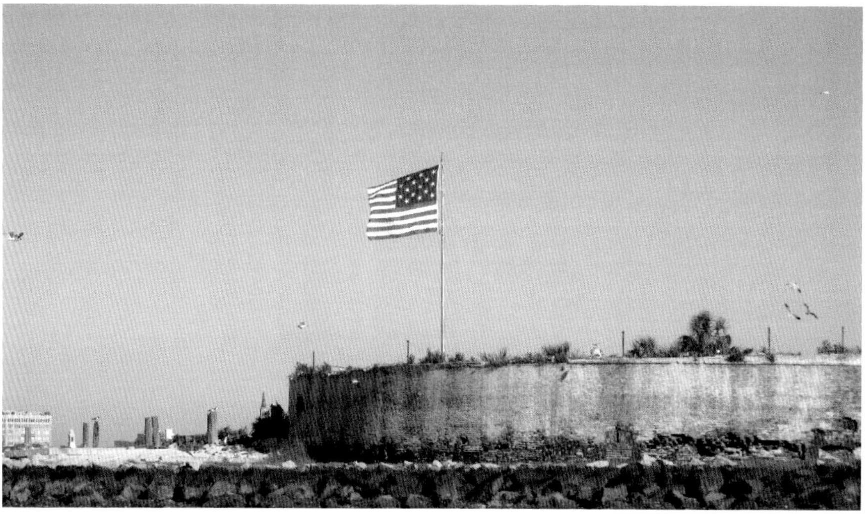

Fort Jefferson. *National Parks Department.*

Stanton then advised the president to commute the sentences of all of the prisoners to life in prison. On July 26, Johnson did just that.

When the prisoners were moved on July 29, in the middle of the night, no one knew where they were headed or why. Neither Mrs. Keys nor Mrs. Stowers were advised of where their husbands were or that they were being moved. It was only through a letter from citizens in Anderson that anyone found out where they were. No one suspected that the president could have had a hand in their removal.

Within five days, President Johnson ordered that they be moved again, this time to Fort Delaware, in Delaware City, Delaware. On August 4, the prisoners arrived on the island.

Life at Fort Jefferson was horrible. With no trees, no plants and nothing but sand around the island, the sun beat down, and the humidity from the sea hurried along the formation of mildew and rot. Flies, mosquitoes and gnats plagued the island and anyone who lived there. It had a well-deserved reputation as America's Devil's Island. For prisoners at Fort Jefferson, especially those sentenced to hard labor, their days were spent on never-ending construction jobs, normally tethered to a ball and chain. Their diet consisted mostly of rotting food and resulted in diarrhea and scurvy. The rest of their daily life included insects, bedbugs, isolation, brutal guards, yellow fever and malaria—all of which came together to make life on the island like a hell on earth.

And while Keys and his group weren't even supposed to be there, it would be some fifty-five days before they were transferred to Fort Delaware.

Life at Fort Delaware wasn't any easier. Some even called it the Andersonville of the North, after the infamous Andersonville prison in southeastern Georgia, where more than thirteen thousand of the forty-five thousand Union prisoners held had died.

Located in the middle of the Delaware River on Pea Patch Island, Fort Delaware had been a prisoner-of-war camp for the Union. The pentagon-shaped building covered six acres on the island and at one time housed more than thirteen thousand Confederate prisoners of war.

Conditions were just as deplorable as at Fort Jefferson. Rotten food, tainted water and overcrowding led to scurvy, smallpox, measles, dysentery, severe malnutrition and death. It is estimated that 2,700 men died at the prison during the war.

While Stanton had wanted the men out of the way and punished, Johnson wanted the men within the reach of the courts. A second battle now raged between Johnson and Secretary of War Stanton as to who had the authority over the prisoners and, indeed, the laws of the country.

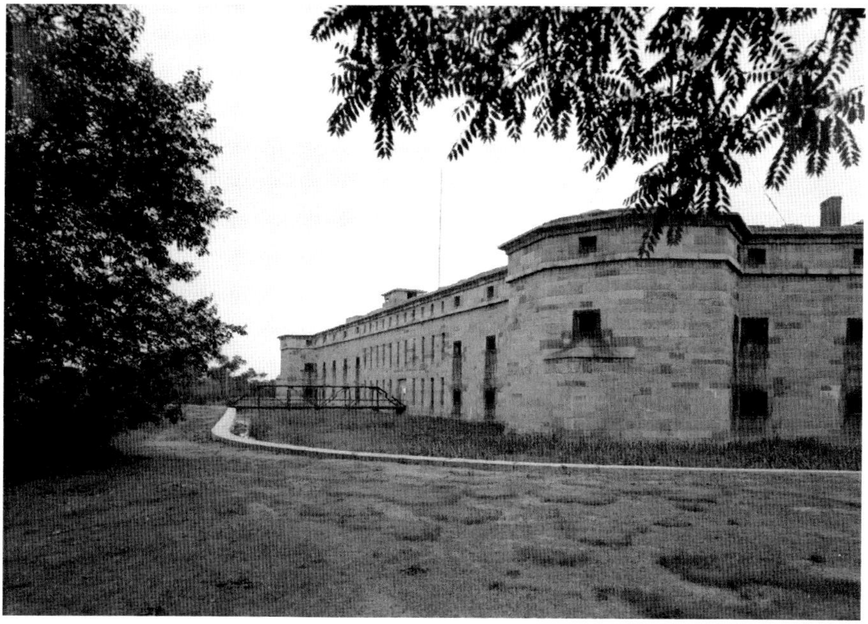

Fort Delaware. *Library of Congress.*

On October 11, the men arrived at Fort Delaware. Lawyers immediately petitioned the court for a writ of habeas corpus. On November 8, Judge Willard Hall of the United States District Court for Delaware, issued the writs of habeas corpus and ordered the prisoners brought before him so that their cases could be heard.

The cases were important ones. At issue wasn't just whether or not four men were being found guilty of murder, but also whether or not the military had a right to try citizens in the southern states in military tribunals, or whether they should have been tried in a civil court. Thousands of other cases depended on this one outcome. Losing this meant that the case would go all the way to the Supreme Court, which would make the final decision.

On November 16, Crawford Keys, Robert Keys and Elisha Byrum entered the court. Gaines Stowers was so sick that he couldn't be moved without endangering his life. Attorneys argued their cases. Attorneys for the military alleged that finding the trial of the men by military tribunal illegal would require finding the entire war unconstitutional. Attorneys for the prisoners compared the military tribunals to "despotic power."

The next day, November 17, Judge Hall made his decision. Because the State of South Carolina was operating as its own government and exercising its civil functions, the military did not have jurisdiction in the case. The war was over. The president had appointed a provisional governor who had reestablished the court system. South Carolina had elected its own governor. The provisional governor had stepped down. In essence, South Carolina was its own state and not subject to military control.

Citing the U.S. Constitution, Hall admonished the military for not being trained in how evidence should be presented in a trial and for denying the prisoners their rights by allowing prejudiced, confusing and perjured testimony in a trial in which the men's lives were at stake. The men were released and returned home.

Upon their arrival in Anderson, crowds of people turned out to greet them. They were received as heroes and honored at a banquet that night at Keys's house. Only Stowers, who was still very sick, was not in attendance.

In Washington, Johnson's actions caught the attention of Congress, which initiated an investigation. The House of Representatives passed a resolution that it would form a select committee to investigate the case, from the murders to the prisoners' release.

During this investigation, Sickles reported to the House of Representatives that the prisoners were at large in Anderson and that no one was doing

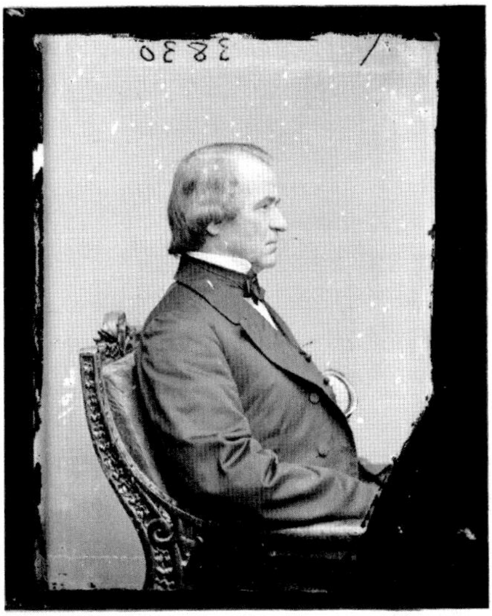

President Andrew Johnson. *National Archives.*

anything to secure them. Attempts to arrest them, he said, were met with signals by the people of Anderson to alert Keys and others that Sickles's men were on the way.

Stanton testified that he only took the actions he did to save the prisoners from execution and to avoid any collusion between the military commanders and the civil authorities in South Carolina. He then took credit for transferring them to Fort Delaware for their health.

The House determined after the proceedings that it was in the best interest of the government to keep the military commissions in place in order to preserve the safety and security of Union forces in the South.

In Anderson, the conflict had its own resolutions.

William Brown, owner of Brown's Ferry, found that he was ostracized by the community and eventually moved away. After forty-five years, he returned to Brown's Ferry but lived on the Georgia side of the river until he committed suicide in July 1916.

Colonel Henry B. Clits, one of the members of the military commission, retired from the army in 1885 with the rank of brigadier general. On October 30, 1888, he registered at the Niagara House in Niagara Falls, New York. At half past five o'clock the next morning, he rose, went downstairs half-dressed, greeted the hotel clerk and left the building. He was never seen again. Many think he committed suicide by jumping into the falls, but there is no evidence his body was ever found. He was sixty-four years old.

Prior to the trial, in 1859, Daniel Sickles had been tried for murder. Edwin Stanton had been his attorney. Sickles had shot Philip Barton Key, district attorney for the District of Columbia and son of Francis Scott Key, for allegedly having an affair with Sickles's wife. Sickles was the first person to use the "not guilty by reason of temporary insanity" plea in a murder trial. Ultimately, he was acquitted and publicly forgave his wife.

After the Brown's Ferry trial, Sickles was appointed to colonel of the Forty-Second U.S. Infantry and, in 1869, he retired as a major general. He later served as U.S. minister to Spain, where he is alleged to have had an affair with Queen Isabella II. After his wife's death, he married a member of the Spanish court. Later, he served as sheriff of New York County and then as a representative of New York in Congress. For many years, he served as chairman of the New York Monuments Commission, until he was found to have embezzled more than $27,000 (about $500,000 in today's money) from the commission.

Sickles died peacefully at the age of ninety-four and was buried in Arlington National Cemetery.

After the Brown's Ferry trial, tensions continued to mount between President Johnson and Secretary of War Stanton. Johnson tried to remove Stanton from office, but Stanton's supporters in Congress passed the Tenure of Office Act, which protected him. Johnson vetoed the bill, but Congress overrode the veto on the same day. Johnson confided in Ulysses Grant that he still wanted to remove Stanton from office. In August 1866, Johnson sent Stanton a letter relieving him of his position and asking him to hand over all of his files to Grant.

In 1868, Congress reinstated Stanton. In February of that year, Johnson informed Congress that he was replacing Stanton with Lorenzo Thomas. Stanton refused to concede his position. That night, the Senate passed a resolution making Stanton's removal illegal, while the House voted to impeach Johnson.

When Grant took office as president in 1869, he appointed Stanton associate justice of the United States Supreme Court. Unfortunately, he died four days after Congress confirmed his nomination.

Crawford Keys continued to live on his farm in Anderson until he turned eighty-six. He died in 1895, just six days before his birthday.

Robert Keys served as an agent of the Southeast Railway Express in Anderson for thirty-five years. He died in 1911. After his release, Gaines Stowers's health continued to decline. He died in 1870.

None of the four men were ever brought to civil court in Anderson County for the murders of the three guards.

8
Manse Jolly

Was he a Confederate hero or a domestic terrorist?

He was six feet, four inches tall, with red hair and a wild, untamed look. And he was out for blood—or so the story goes.

Manson Sherill Jolly was Anderson's own one-man army, bent on serving up his own brand of justice as revenge for the deaths of his brothers in the Civil War. Portrayed as a tortured soul who just wanted life to return to the way it was before the war, Jolly was an antihero before antiheroes were a thing.

Or he was a braggart and a violent man who slaughtered innocent men just trying to do their jobs.

One thing is sure: Manse Jolly is Anderson County's most infamous local legend.

According to legend and some factual accounts, Manse Jolly was born in the Lebanon area of Anderson County, between Anderson and Pendleton, before the Civil War. He could read and write. He and his brothers helped his widowed mother with their 240-acre farm until the war started. Jolly joined the Confederate army as a scout in the First South Carolina Calvary, Company F. Six of his brothers enlisted with him.

When the war ended, Jolly and his friend Tom Largent made their way back from Virginia to Anderson. When he got home, he learned that five of his brothers had been killed in the war. He vowed then and there to take five Union lives for each of his brothers' lives.

Manse, Tom, Manse's mother and Manse's two sisters worked to bring the farm back to its former glory. But not too long after Manse and Tom returned, they were assessed with a $192 tax (nearly $3,000 today) for reparations.

According to *Manse: One Man's War*, a biography written by Wilton Earle, Manse and Tom headed to the hills to gather up cattle that had scattered from the destroyed or abandoned farms in the area. They would bring the cattle into Anderson, sell them and then use the money to pay taxes. But Manse was upset by the number of Union soldiers in Anderson, which he saw as an occupying force.

On the night of January 20, 1866, according to the *Greenville News*, Jolly rode down Fant Street, hooting and hollering and shooting his gun. The camp of Union forces in the town spilled out of their tents to see what they assumed was a whole battalion of rebels. Instead, it was just Jolly. After he rode through the camp, the Union soldiers gathered themselves enough to give chase. But, legend has it, they never caught him.

And that was Jolly's style.

Come try to find him at his house and disturb his mother and sister? He'd kill as many Union forces guarding the house as he could, firing on them from the woods with his rifle. Send three young black Union soldiers into the fields of his family farm to arrest him? He'd make sure they were never seen or heard from again, but plow his fields with horses branded with "U.S." on their hindquarters. Send three white troopers up to Pendleton to see what they could find out about him? He'd talk with them for a while, standing there in the square, then he'd tell them who he was and shoot them all dead.

Make a broad announcement in a bar in downtown Anderson about how you're going to hand Jolly his hat and then hand him over to Washington? Better know who is in the bar before Jolly walks right up to you, tells you who he is, points a gun at you and tells you to leave the bar or die trying.

Jolly was known for brash behavior, ungodly amounts of courage and a fierce allegiance to his family. At one point, the legend goes, a band of Union soldiers decided that the best time to get Jolly would be during the dark of night, when he couldn't see to shoot so well. So, they headed up the road from Anderson to Jolly's house in hopes of catching him unawares.

As the men talked among themselves on the long walk, the conversation turned to Jolly—what they thought of him, how they were going to catch him, where they thought their best chances of getting him were.

No one noticed the tall, lanky soldier who fell in with them. In the dark, it was hard to make out features. He laughed when they did, asked questions about the mission and listened to every word they said. It wasn't until the road turned and the bank fell off into woods that the stranger disappeared. Moments later, the band of men found themselves under attack. Jolly was shooting at them from the woods. Having listened to every word they'd said as he walked with them, he fired on the soldiers in the moonlight until they all decided it was best to turn around and head back home.

When his brother died in a robbery, Jolly swore that another one hundred men would die. And he didn't get too far off the mark. He found the men responsible for his brother's death, tracked them and killed them, as well as several innocent bystanders.

Jolly has been held responsible for some 123 killings. It could have been more, might have been less. It's hard to tell, since every unsolved killing of anyone remotely connected with the Union is attributed to Jolly.

As a show of strength and commitment, Jolly allegedly once rode into downtown Anderson wearing a Union army uniform and hid within a company of Union soldiers while they stood in formation. As Major Lowell Bartow, a Union hero brought to Anderson to find and capture Jolly, began to speak, Jolly tried to shoot him. When he missed, Jolly escaped through back alleys with the help of Anderson supporters. Bartow put the town under martial law and placed a $5,000 bounty on Manse's head, then raised it to $7,500. In today's terms, that would be a bit over $113,000.

After supposedly killing a tax collector, Jolly decided to go after Bartow. According to Earle's book *Manse*, Jolly tracked Bartow to a whorehouse, set the house on fire and shot the men and women as they came out, with the assistance of fledgling Klansmen. After that, Jolly left town. He hid out in the mountains for a while before heading out on horseback for Texas. There he met up with a former Confederate soldier, now a ranch owner, and was given shelter and a job. When Jolly fell in love with the rancher's daughter, the two married.

Tragically, Jolly died, not at the hands of a Union soldier, as in a romantic novel, but in the swollen banks of the flooded Red River in Texas, trying to get home to his wife.

Stories of Jolly are conflicting, though, and they changed over the years. In the 1930s, Manse Jolly was portrayed as a soft-hearted but cold-blooded killer, just out for justice for his family. In the 1950s, much of the narrative had to do with Manse being mad at the number of black soldiers put in charge of Anderson. In a story printed in the *Greenwood Index-Journal* in 1956,

Manse went to help a neighbor who was dealing with ex-slaves who had stolen from him and "Negro" troops who wouldn't do anything about it. In the story, he strung up an ex-slave and beat him for stealing. But the ex-slave ran to the "Negro" colonel in Anderson and complained. The troops came for Manse, but Jolly dispatched them in his own way.

As late as 1967, a former statesman told the *Index-Journal* of his time as Manse Jolly's boy bodyguard, standing watch at his father's house while Jolly slept the few hours he could without fear of Union capture.

While Jolly's home still stands on Manse Jolly Road, there are tales that when the well on his land was cleaned out, Union buttons, buckles and brass were found among the debris. Could bodies have been thrown in that well?

Manse Jolly was a legend who lived in Anderson County, but whether the tales of his rebel justice are to be believed is still up for debate. One thing is certain: stories of his life and exploits won't soon be forgotten.

9
P.A. Wilhite and the Ether Frolics

Surgery in the 1860s wasn't nearly as comfortable as it is today. Without anesthetic, surgery was a painful, sometimes deadly experience. Patients sometimes were given whiskey to dull the pain, but other than the numbing produced by a few stiff belts, the patient felt everything the doctor was doing.

According to the descendants of one Anderson family, a doctor in Anderson County was responsible for the discovery of ether as an anesthetic. But the history books show us that the identity of the doctor responsible for bringing anesthesia to the operating table is still in dispute.

Let's take a look at the state of medicine in the nineteenth century.

In the mid-1800s, many of the drugs now banned as controlled substances were commonly prescribed by physicians or used as ingredients in drinks and elixirs. For instance, in 1832, opium was commonly used as an ingredient in patent medicines. Patent medicines were nineteenth-century concoctions composed of ingredients like vegetable extracts and simple herbs mixed with ample doses of alcohol or other drugs. Advertisements claimed that these elixirs could cure most anything—from venereal disease to tuberculosis, colic in infants, constipation and "female complaints."

Without a doubt, these elixirs did nothing to cure anything, but they did help to introduce cocaine and opium to proper society. Throughout the 1800s, opiates like morphine and opium were widely distributed in patent medicines. In addition, physicians were in the habit of prescribing opiates for menstrual and menopausal disorders. Women became the prevalent class of opiate addicts. While women would not be seen in public drinking alcohol, the patent medicines provided a convenient, gentle drug suitable for a lady of decorum.

It was also during this time that cocaine was a commonly prescribed medicine. Discovered in 1844, when it was isolated from the coca leaves, cocaine didn't get much attention until 1883, when Dr. Theodor Aschenbrandt, a German army physician, issued a supply of pure cocaine to Bavarian soldiers during maneuvers. Aschenbrandt later reported that the drug helped soldiers endure fatigue during battle-like conditions.

In 1884, Sigmund Freud was reported to have tried cocaine and later prescribed it to a friend to help with his friend's addiction to morphine. Freud also reportedly sent cocaine to his fiancée to "make her more lively." After writing essays about how wonderful the drug was, Freud is also thought to have periodically used it himself to relieve his depression.

By 1885, John Styth Pemberton of Atlanta, Georgia, was set on introducing to the public his "French Wine Coca—Ideal Nerve and Tonic Stimulant." His previous forays into patent medicines had such names as Triplex Liver Pills and Glove of Flour Cough Syrup. This new product, however, relied heavily on the extract of coca leaves. Pemberton, a pharmacist, patterned his new elixir off of French coca wine, which was Bordeaux wine laced with the extract of coca leaves. Pemberton substituted extracts from the kola nut in a sugary syrup instead of the wine. While the kola nut extract added a jolt from caffeine, the coca extract added a jolt of cocaine.

In its first year of production, Pemberton reportedly sold twenty-five gallons of the syrup. Advertised as a "remarkable therapeutic agent" and as a "sovereign remedy," his Coca-Cola syrup was considered a cure for a long list of problems, from melancholy to insomnia.

It wouldn't be until 1906, when the federal government passed pure food and drug laws, that Pemberton's successors, who were still making Coca-Cola, would switch from using coca leaves to a "decocainized" version of the extract.

It was also in the early 1900s that the federal government began restricting the use of narcotics and other drugs through controlled substances laws.

In the mid-1800s, though, ether was considered a party drug. A colorless liquid, ether causes unconsciousness. It was discovered in 1275, and its hypnotic effects were documented as early as 1540 by a German botanist and chemist, Valerius Cordus. The drug was also noted to produce sleep. In 1794, ether began its use as a medical treatment and gained notoriety as a recreational drug. Starting in the 1830s, "ether frolics" were held, usually

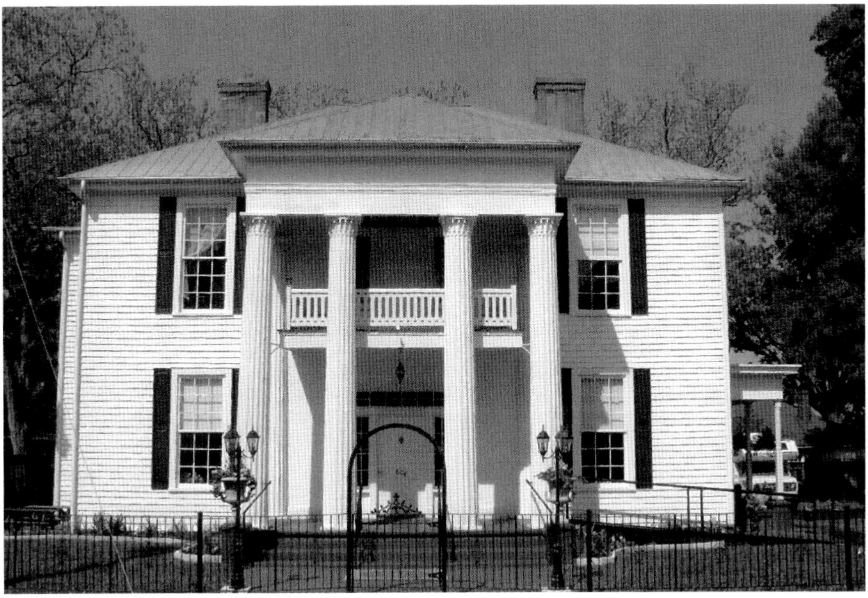

The Wilhite House, circa 1980. *South Carolina Department of Archives and History.*

by medical students, in which participants inhaled ether to experience its euphoric effects. But at higher doses, ether can render one unconscious.

That's where Anderson physician P.A. Wilhite comes in. In 1876, Dr. Wilhite consulted renowned New York City physician Dr. Martin Sims about his daughter. Wilhite told Sims that his daughter needed to undergo surgery but that she should be sedated first with ether. Sims initially balked at the idea, until Wilhite told him that not only had he assisted in the first surgery using ether, but also that he had participated in several others as a medical student in the early 1840s. Sims didn't believe Wilhite. It was Sims's knowledge that the first surgery with anesthesia had been performed in Boston in 1846. Wilhite begged to differ.

Philip Abney Wilhite was born in 1822 in Elberton, Georgia. By the age of nineteen, he was a medical student working with Dr. Crawford W. Long in Jefferson, Georgia.

Wilhite told Sims that, in 1839, he had attended a quilting party at a Mr. Ware's house outside of Athens, Georgia, with several young men and women. The quilting ended in an "ether frolic." During the fun, the group spied a twelve-year-old slave boy at the door. Since he was enjoying watching the frolic, the group asked if he'd like to come in and try some ether.

The boy refused. Wilhite and another man then grabbed the boy and held him down while Wilhite poured ether onto a rag and held it over the boy's face. Even though the boy fought furiously, the two men restrained him and kept the cloth firmly covering his nose and mouth. After a long struggle, the boy became passive and quiet. Wilhite and his accomplice released the boy. But to their surprise, he didn't get up and start acting the fool like the rest of them had. He laid there, his breathing labored, unresponsive to the calls and pokes of the others. Instead of inducing euphoria, the drug had anesthetized him to the point of unconsciousness. Fearing the boy had died, Wilhite worked to revive him. When his efforts failed, the partygoers panicked. Wilhite sent a horse and rider for the nearest physician. The young ladies present at the party fled the scene, fearing the boy had been murdered.

When the closest physician, a Dr. Reese, who lived five miles away, arrived and woke the boy with the usual methods—he poured water on his face, slapped him, raised him up and shook him violently—the young man eventually came around. He had suffered no ill effects and had no recollection of the painful means in which the partygoers had tried to arouse him. Dr. Reese mentioned to Wilhite that he had never seen such a thing before. Wilhite told Sims that he had known that the ether had this effect since the age of ten. He also told Sims that he thought Dr. Crawford Long had gotten the idea for ether as an anesthetic from Wilhite's retelling of the incident.

Dr. Long was also a participant in "ether frolics" at the time and noticed that when participants suffered from minor injuries or bruising while under the influence of ether, they felt no pain from them. At this time, there were few surgical procedures available. Without knowledge of how to satisfactorily administer anesthesia to put the patient into a deep sleep or to numb areas of the body, doctors had to perform surgeries hurriedly.

Some anesthesia was available, such as alcohol, hashish and opium derivatives. Additionally, physicians used some physical methods of producing an insensitivity to pain, including packing a limb in ice or applying a tourniquet to it. Still other forms of anesthesia were available for knocking out the patients—namely, physically knocking them out via a blow to the head or through strangulation. More often than not, however, the patient was simply restrained by physical force, thus making surgery a last resort.

But as more and more information was revealed about the human body and surgical procedures, doctors realized there was a need to find safe methods of preventing pain in patients. The advent of professional dentistry added to this need. Because of the sensitivity of the teeth, mouth and gums, dentists had an urgent need to treat their patients' pain.

Wilhite told Sims that he had mentioned the incident with the young slave boy to Dr. Long. But Long said later that Wilhite had not been in Jefferson at that time and that he never helped Long with surgery, not as an assistant or even as an observer. Long did, however, conclude that ether could be used to provide patients with pain-free surgery. It wasn't long before Long had convinced James Venable, a student in nearby Athens, to undergo surgery while under the influence of ether.

Crawford Long was born in 1815 in Danielsville, Georgia. By the age of fourteen, he had exhausted the academic resources of his local academy and applied to the University of Georgia. There he received his associate's degree in medicine before moving to Lexington, Kentucky, and attending Transylvania University to complete his medical training. He studied under a renowned surgeon of the day, Benjamin Dudley. Long found the surgeries to be harrowing experiences, as patients weren't sedated and often suffered excruciating pain.

After a year at Transylvania, Long transferred to the University of Pennsylvania in Philadelphia, where he was able to study with some of the greatest medical scholars of the day and witness new medical techniques firsthand. Long graduated with a medical degree in 1839 and, after a hospital internship, returned to Georgia to take over a rural medical practice in 1841.

About the same time that Wilhite mentioned the incident with the boy to Long, Long began to experiment with sulfuric ether and nitrous oxide as anesthetics. He performed his first surgical procedure on March 30, 1842, removing a tumor from the neck of James Venable. Over the next several years, he would perform more surgeries using ether and eventually began to use it in his obstetrical practice. But he didn't publish his findings.

At the time, anesthetics were viewed with skepticism by both the medical profession and the general public. Doctors felt that the use of gases or other chemicals during surgery would not provide pain relief, while some Jefferson, Georgia residents believed that Long was engaging in witchcraft and disturbing the natural order of things—pain, in this instance, being God's natural way of cleansing the soul.

Years went by. In 1846, an editorial in *Medical Examiner* touched on William Morton, a dentist in Boston who claimed to have used ether as an anesthetic. In January of the following year, the same journal published several articles about ether experiments.

Long, hoping to get the recognition of his peers and to help the medical field, began writing his own account of his discovery. He presented his findings to the Medical College of Georgia in Augusta in 1849. But by that time, two other doctors, Horace Wells and Charles Jackson, claimed to be the discoverers of surgical anesthesia.

P.A. Wilhite wanted some of that credit, too. In 1852, he graduated from medical college in Charleston, and moved to Anderson, where he practiced medicine and surgery until his death in 1892. Before he died, though, he testified in the *Proceedings of the Medical Association of South Carolina* that he administered ether to the young slave boy at the party in 1841. The participants at the frolic who had restrained the twelve-year-old boy testified to the events and to the date of 1841.

Wilhite also gave interviews to the *Atlanta Daily Constitution* to detail the events and his relationship to Long's use of ether as an anesthetic.

Until 2017, a sign in front of the Wilhite Mansion on the corner of McDuffie and River Streets proclaimed the building as the "Historic Wilhite House, home of P.A. Wilhite, the discoverer of ether."

For years, there was controversy over who discovered the anesthetic qualities of ether. Wilhite claimed he discovered ether's properties, while Long claimed he was the first to use the gas as an anesthetic in surgery. Others claimed they were the first to use ether as an anesthetic in documented surgery.

But Wilhite didn't use the gas until he began his own practice in Anderson. Long never wrote about his surgery or his findings until after he read about someone else's account. Wells was a dentist, and it was thought he used nitrous oxide, not ether, during his procedure.

Morton and Jackson administered their ether to patients of other surgeons at the prestigious Massachusetts General Hospital, but not until 1846, two years after Long had used the gas on Venable.

The last word was given by the National Eclectic Medical Association, a late nineteenth-century organization that advocated for the best medical remedies. It passed a resolution declaring that Long was the discoverer of anesthesia. Since that time, Long has been recognized worldwide as the discoverer of anesthesia and has been memorialized with monuments, statues, paintings, and a U.S. postage stamp. A museum in his honor stands at the site of his medical practice in Jefferson. Wilhite's assistance in Long's discovery is not mentioned at the museum.

In the end, none of the men involved in the controversy fared well, except for Dr. Wilhite. Long died after delivering a baby. He was living in poverty brought on by the Civil War and is said to have worked himself to death to provide for his family. Dr. Horace Wells went insane and committed suicide in New York City in 1848. The insanity was said to arise partly from the anesthesia controversy, even though he is thought to have used nitrous oxide instead.

Morton died in New York City as well, in 1868. The cause of death was listed as "congestion of the brain" after an episode of erratic behavior in which he threw himself from his buggy into a lake near Central Park then returned to his buggy, racing furiously for a short distance before jumping over a fence and falling into a stupor. He died a short time later at St. Luke's Hospital in New York City.

Dr. Charles Jackson resided for a long time in an insane asylum and was believed to be incurable, his insanity stemming from his part in the controversy.

Only Wilhite seems to have fared well in later life. He went on to have a happy and successful life in Anderson. He married Cora Lavinia Hilley in

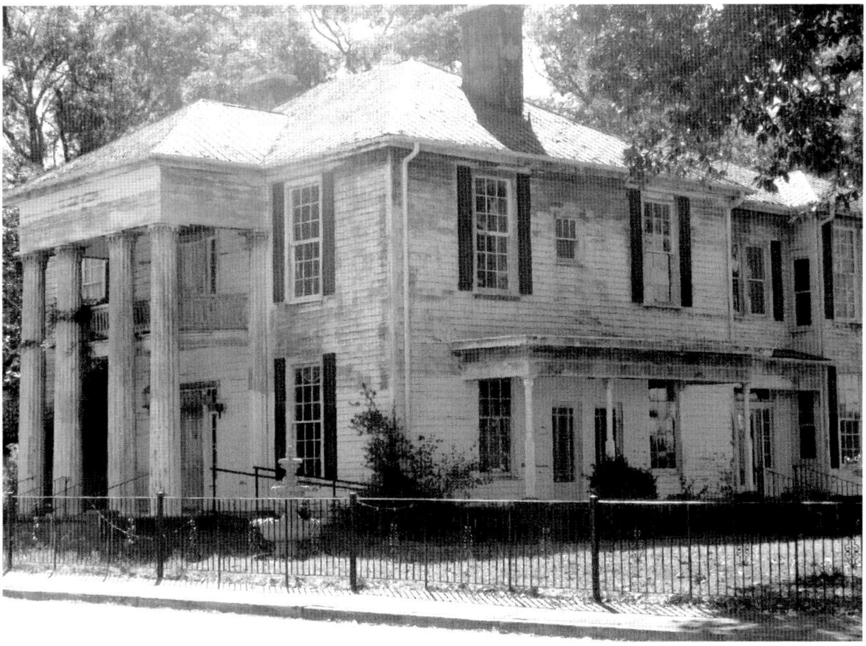

Wilhite House, 2016. *Author's collection.*

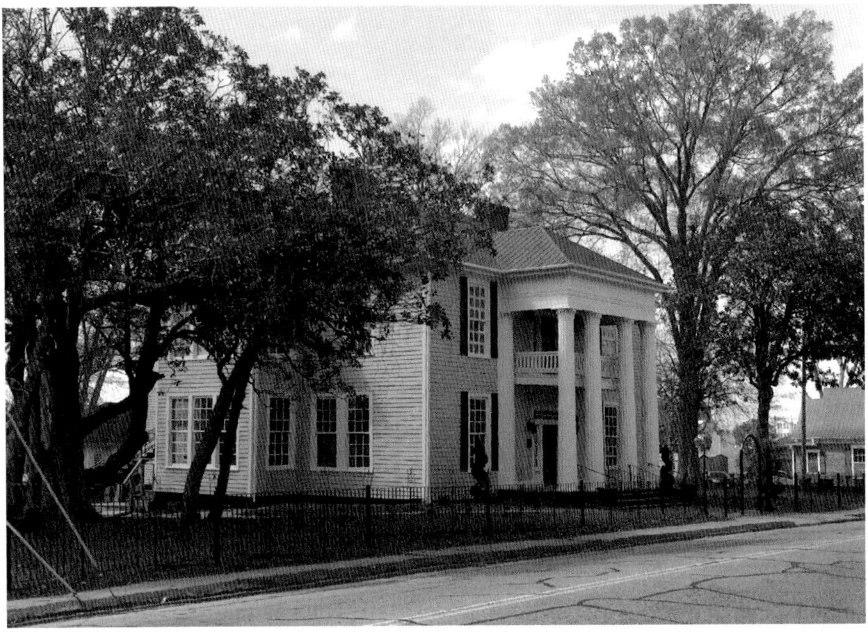

Modern Wilhite House, 2017. *Author's collection.*

1847, and they had four children, one of whom, Joseph Oliver Wilhite, went on to become a doctor. Two other children, Turner Frank Wilhite and Cora Wilhite Baker, both died in their twenties. Mary Margaret Wilhite never married and died at the age of eighty-eight, the last member of the family to live in the family home, a six-thousand-square-foot building erected in 1858. As a doctor, Wilhite treated both Union and Confederate soldiers during the Civil War, and it is thought that this fact may be one reason why his house was not destroyed during the war.

In 2016, Bob Hall purchased the Wilhite House and proceeded to renovate it. In 2017, the work was completed. Hall and his business partner had to replace everything in the house, from the plumbing to the electrical work. Although they did find a lot of the property in disrepair, Hall said they didn't find much in the way of surprise, outside of a few newspapers from the 1960s stuffed in a fireplace.

The house was used briefly as a place for social gatherings before being placed on the market in 2017 as a single-family home.

Part III

THE MODERN ERA

10

Electricity and the Electric City

In the late 1880s, a war was brewing among some scientists, and Anderson, the first electrified city in the South, was on the periphery of it.

At the time, Thomas Edison and Nikola Tesla were battling it out over which electrical current worked better, direct current or alternating current.

In the 1870s, outdoor lighting started popping up in American cities. Using alternating current (AC), the lights, called arc lighting, were intensely bright and extremely high voltage. Overhead lines were able to run power from generators up to seven miles away and supply enough power to light up the streetlights of a whole city. But getting the power inside homes was a different story.

Thomas Edison believed the secret to supplying power to homes and businesses, as well as to streetlights, lay in direct current (DC). Edison's electrical system relied on low power (110 volts) running through homes, enough to power up the incandescent light bulb he had designed specifically for the system. Edison's method also incorporated electric meters, which allowed customers to be billed based on the amount of power they used. The drawback to Edison's system, though, was that, at 110 volts, the power couldn't travel more than a mile from the generator, leaving cities with the need for multiple power stations or power only for certain neighborhoods.

On the other end of the spectrum lay Nikola Tesla, a brilliant Serbian immigrant who felt that alternating current could power houses and neighborhood businesses as well as it did outdoor street lamps.

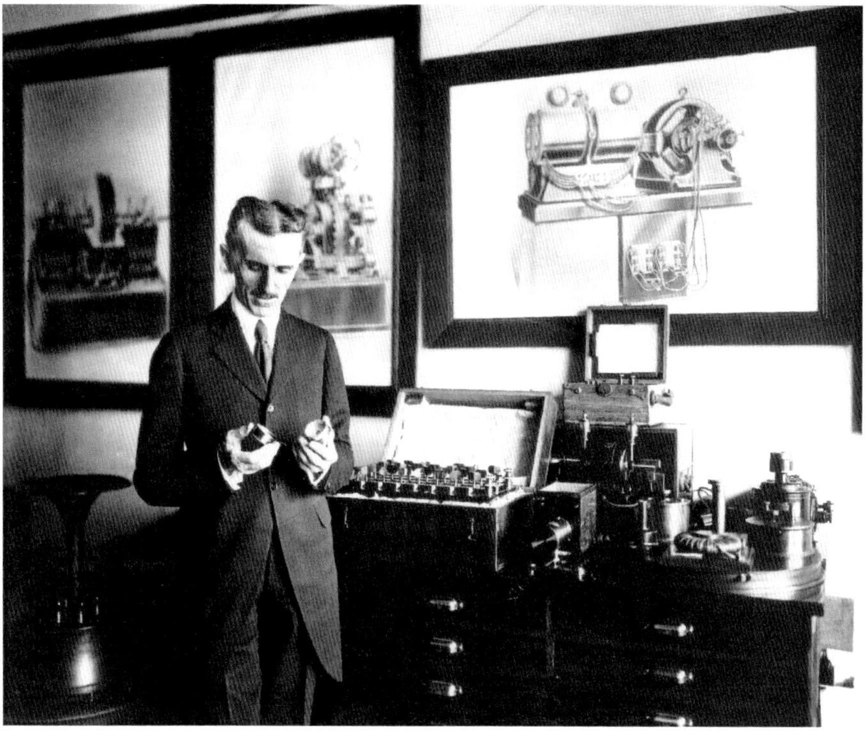

Nikola Tesla. *Library of Congress.*

Tesla had worked at one time in Edison's Parisian power plants. In 1884, he immigrated to America, hoping to work for Edison, who was then his idol. After a few days in America, Tesla learned that one of Edison's engines, installed on the SS *Oregon*, had failed and that Edison and his company were struggling to get it fixed in time for the ship to set sail. Tesla volunteered to help and pulled an all-nighter until he and a crew had fixed the ship and set it sailing. After that, Edison hired the twenty-eight-year-old engineer and set him to work for the Edison Company.

Things wouldn't be smooth sailing for Tesla, though. For a few months, Tesla worked for Edison, coming in at 10:00 a.m. and leaving sometimes as late as 5:00 a.m. the next morning, helping the company with its problems. At one point, Tesla said, Edison promised him $50,000 (the equivalent of $1,250,000 today) if he could come up with workable upgrades to the company's generators. He came up with twenty-four of them. But Edison told Tesla he'd been joking and that, when Tesla became a real American, he'd get the joke.

Tesla resigned.

And that's when the war started. Tesla advocated AC, which meant fewer power plants and more efficiency. Edison advocated DC, mostly because his light bulbs and other inventions were based on it. The two fought it out through public relations, the court of public opinion and legislation. (Edison and his advocates even helped pass legislation that the electric chair must be operated by AC, leaving the public horrified at the destructive power of the high voltage!)

Around that same time, in Anderson, William Church Whitner had just graduated, for the second time, from the University of South Carolina and was working as a railroad engineer. The young man came down with typhoid fever and was forced to recuperate in his father's house in Anderson. By 1889, the Town of Anderson had hired him to build a power plant and the accompanying waterworks system. But, once the steam-powered plant was complete, it was too expensive to build and operate the waterworks.

Whitner went back to the drawing board and played with the idea of using Tesla's alternating current theory as it applied to river water. The Seneca River was just outside of town. Combining the reach of AC with the natural energy of turbulent river water seemed like a natural fit. Whitner traveled to New York City to get advice from Tesla on how to construct the generator for such a system.

In 1894, Whitner returned to Anderson and started building his power plant. Leasing a portion of McFall's Mill, a flour- and gristmill on the Rocky River, Whitner began building his five-thousand-volt alternating current generator using Tesla's ideas. The next year, the generator was ready to start. On May 1, 1895, businessmen and community leaders gathered at the mill to see either the greatest power achievement in the Upstate or Whitner's folly fail to work.

But it did work. Power from the generator traveled six miles from the water system pumps to a power station in Anderson on Tribble Street. It was the first time anyone had successfully sent electrical transmissions over a long distance in the South. Because of the success, Whitner was able to find financing to build a larger generator at Portman Shoals, eleven miles west of the original mill, on the Seneca River. Whitner's company, Anderson Water, Light and Power Company, built a ten-thousand-volt generator and the accompanying buildings. On November 1, 1897, the generator went into operation and was the nation's first hydroelectric facility to generate power without step-up transformers. The generator fed power into homes, onto city streets, into businesses and into the Anderson water system. Because of Whitner's invention, and his endless supply of power, the Charleston *News and Courier* named Anderson the "Electric City."

Portman Shoals also powered the South's only electric cotton gin. Starting in 1897, the gin was the first in the country—and quite possibly the world—to be powered by electricity. Owned by Oliver "Duck" Bolt, the gin was located on Bolt's three-hundred-acre farm about three miles west of Anderson.

Bolt was said to be a hardworking man who never went to school but managed to learn to read and write. Although he lived in Anderson for a short time, he spent more than forty years working his farm, living in a log cabin he built on his property. For most of his working years, Bolt was said to own only one shirt, which was washed each day and laid to dry before the fireplace at night.

In 1886, things began to look up for Bolt, though. He built a two-story, ten-room frame house and expanded his farm to incorporate a steam-powered cotton gin, a gristmill and a wheat thrasher. When Whitner's power reached Anderson, Bolt was the first farmer in the country to contract with Anderson Water, Light and Power to have his gin run by electricity.

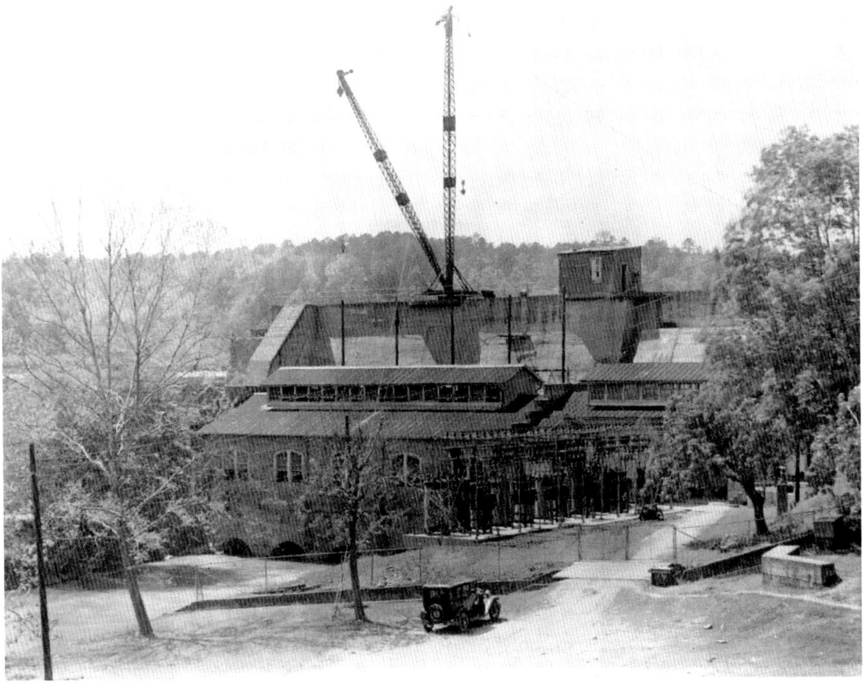

Portman Shoals Dam under construction. *Courtesy of South Carolinian Library, University of South Carolina, Columbia, South Carolina.*

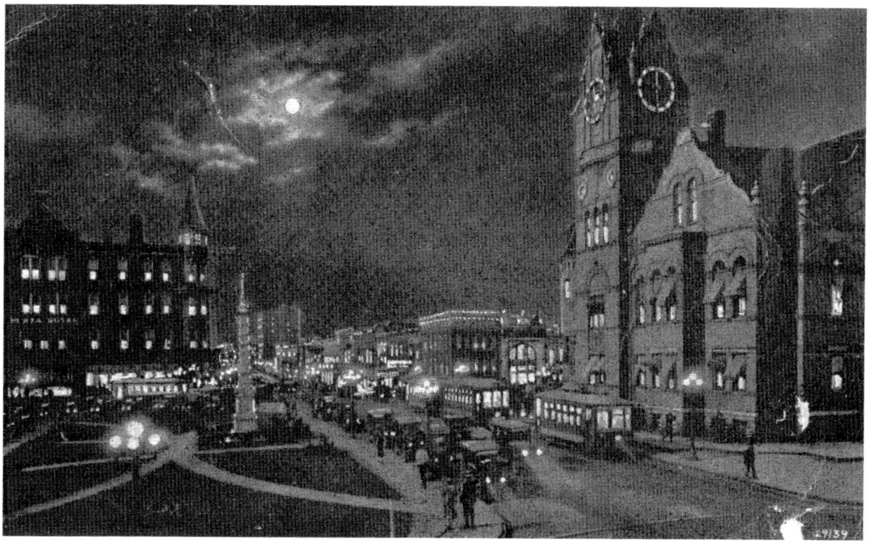

A postcard of downtown Anderson, circa 1910. *Author's collection.*

The power plant supplied power to all of Anderson until December 1901, when a flood destroyed Portman Shoals dam and its generators. For more than nine months, the city returned to the dark until the generator could be rebuilt. In September 1902, the power returned, and life with electricity was restored to the city.

Buoyed by his success, Whitner went on to develop hydroelectric power systems for other communities, including Columbus, Griffin and Elberton, Georgia. Across the South, hydroelectric power was turning on the lights.

One of Whitner's employees, William States Lee, and a financial partner, Dr. W. Gill Wylie, worked to build a plant on the Catawba River in York County. However, the Catawba plant ran into financial difficulties and Whitner left the plant, choosing to move on to a position with the Virginia Railway and Power Company in Richmond, Virginia. Wylie, however, continued with the project and found the money to complete the generator.

Using Whitner's original design, Wylie approached James B. Duke, one of his patients, about the hydroelectric plant. Duke bought into the idea and funded the plant, starting what is now known as Duke Energy, one of the largest power companies in the country, in the process.

While Edison continued to bad-mouth Tesla's ideas, Whitner was able to prove them true and to show that the possibilities were endless. Powering the South, Whitner helped move the needle toward alternating current across the country—a move that the rest of the nation eventually followed. Tesla partnered with George Westinghouse—who himself had been feuding with Edison for years—and the two were able to use alternating current to build a power plant at Niagara Falls to power New York City. The resulting power grid is similar to the same system we use today.

As an aside, Edison's point about homes not being able to handle the high voltage of alternating current still stands. Even our modern homes are not capable of handling the voltage of AC, which is why most home-based devices convert the current before it enters the home. That's what the big square thing on the back of your laptop is doing. Studies are still being conducted to see if there isn't a way to effectively and efficiently use them together.

Fires and floods continually assaulted the generators at Portman Shoals in their early years. New ones were built in their place. Beginning in 1911, generators were built to transmit power to the city. The generators operated at 225 revolutions per minute and produced 2,300 volts and 303 amps per terminal. Portman Shoals was shut down on December 9, 1960, to make way for the incoming waters of Hartwell Lake. The generator was moved to downtown Anderson and, in 2008, placed in Generator Park,

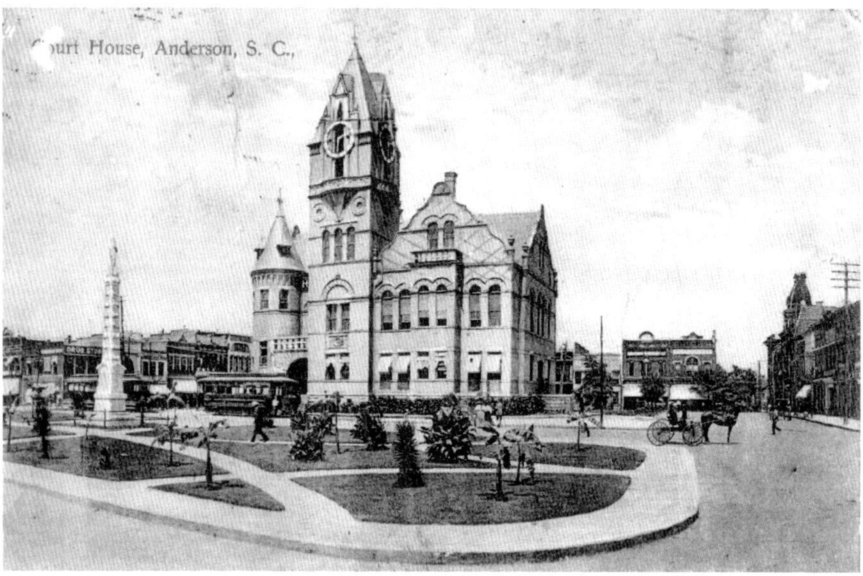

A postcard of Anderson Court House Square, circa early 1900s. *Courtesy of South Caroliniana Library, University of South Carolina, Columbia, South Carolina.*

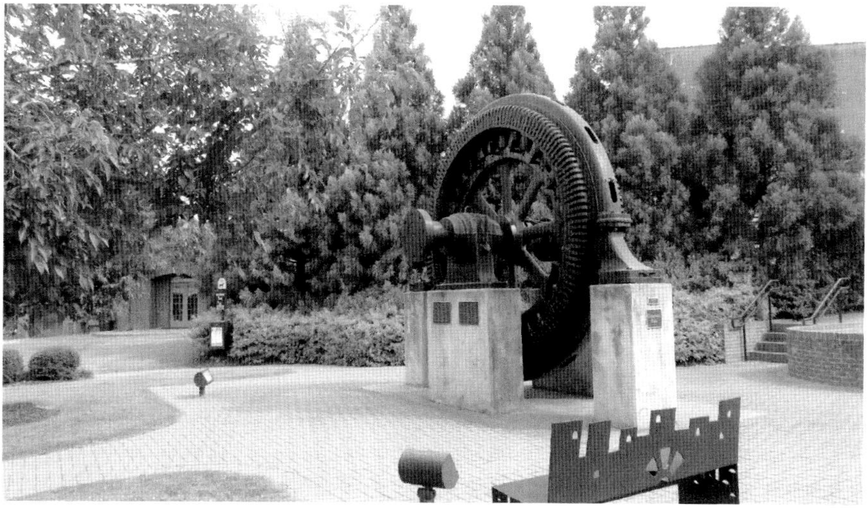

The wheel from Portman Shoals Dam in Generator Park in downtown Anderson. *Author's collection.*

located at the corner of Whitner and McDuffie Streets, by a group called TBA (To Benefit Anderson).

Just up the street, a life-sized statue of William Church Whitner stands, holding his watch and looking up at the streetlight on that historic day when his dream turned the lights on in Anderson.

11

Maud Broadwick

South Carolina's First Aerial Death

In 1905, Anderson, like many small towns in America, found its most exotic entertainment in traveling circuses and shows.

One traveling entertainment group brought more than smiles and laughter to Anderson: it brought death, possibly by suicide or murder.

There was little entertainment in 1905 for the average resident of Anderson. Think about it. No televisions. Radios weren't a household fixture and were primarily used to communicate with ships at sea. Movies were in their infancy, and most of what was being produced were silent, one-reel movies featuring little in the way of stories. The entertainment of the day was books, records, music in the home and visits with friends. So, when a circus came to town, it was big news—and a big draw for crowds from near and far.

In November 1905, Riddle's Southern Circus came to Anderson, bringing with it the headlining act of Charles and Maud Broadwick, aeronauts with a huge hot-air balloon. Since the Wright brothers had flown their airplane only two years before, anything that had to do with flight was a big draw. The Broadwicks' act was guaranteed to please and amaze all who came to see it.

In those days, Anderson was home to Buena Vista Park. Located off River Street, near White Street, the park was a tree-lined escape on the outskirts of the city. Owned by the Anderson Traction Company, the local streetcar line, Buena Vista Park was an entertainment complex that provided Anderson residents with plenty to do on the weekends. Since mills didn't operate on

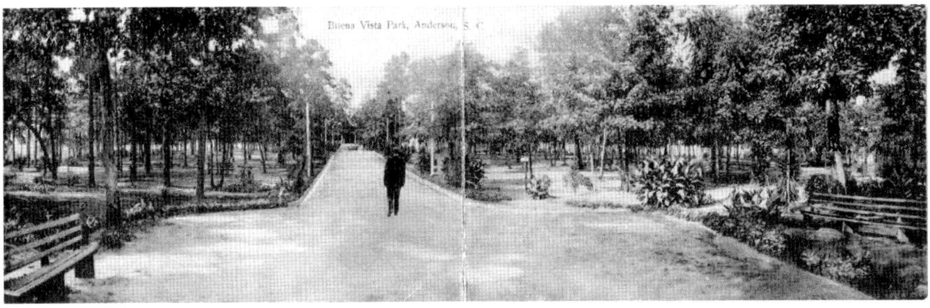

Buena Vista Park in its heyday. *Courtesy of South Caroliniana Library, University of South Carolina, Columbia, South Carolina.*

the weekends, the streetcars and trolleys sat idle on Saturdays and Sundays with no millworkers to transport back and forth. So, the trolley company built Buena Vista Park, with swimming pools, a theater, a baseball field, a zoo, restaurants, a dance pavilion and other attractions. Residents used the trolleys to get back and forth to the park, providing the streetcars with something to do on the weekends—and a way to make money every day of the week.

During the week of November 2, 1905, the Broadwicks' act was the show to see. Riddle's circus took up most of the park, and the Broadwick act included their signature aeronautic exercise—a hot-air balloon rising into the air with Maud Broadwick on a trapeze under the basket of the balloon. Once the balloon reached about two hundred to three hundred feet, the partner on the ground would fire a gun to let the partner in the air know it was time to descend. Then, with a parachute, the performer on the trapeze would jump, release the parachute and fall to the ground. Pretty simple compared to modern entertainment, but at the time, the idea of rising into the skies and falling back again, slowed by a sheet, was extraordinary.

Even before the show began, though, there were rumblings that something was wrong. Witnesses that day told officials that the Broadwicks had gotten into a rather loud fight in front of circus-goers and carnival workers prior to their act, and Mrs. Broadwick seemed terribly distraught.

Not much is known about the Broadwicks, especially Maud. Charles Broadwick was originally John Murray, having changed his name for the stage. Both of them were from Cincinnati, Ohio. Not much is known about when they were married, but what is known is that the parents of twenty-year-old Maud were not in favor of the marriage, and that Maud was estranged from her parents over it.

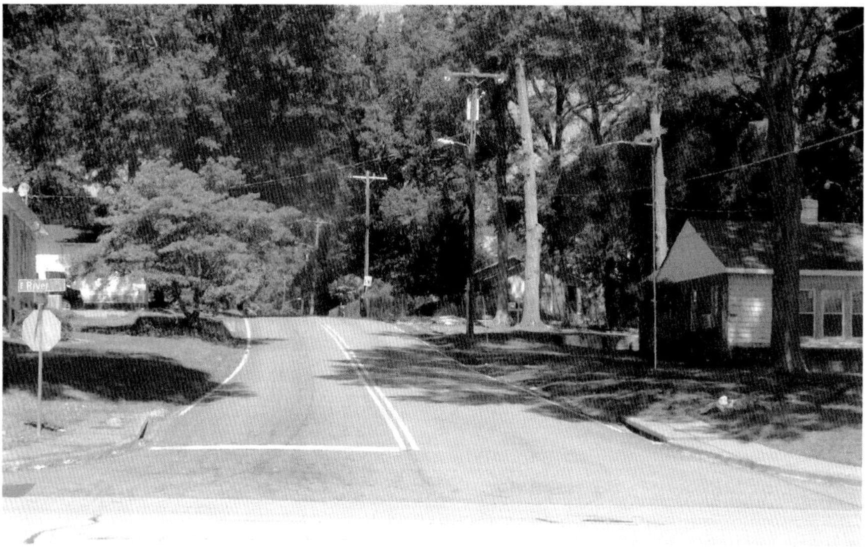

The road to Buena Vista Park today. *Author's collection.*

On the afternoon of November 3, as Maud prepared for their act, her husband approached her. No one heard what he said to her, but one witness overheard Maud tell Charles, "This will be my last ascension!"

Taking her place on the trapeze, Maud gave the signal to let the balloon go. The circus strongmen who had been holding the balloon released it. But immediately, it was clear something was wrong. Maud's arm was tangled in her parachute, and she began to call for help. Charles Broadwick and the others did the only thing they could do, hold on to her. But when they reached for her, it caused the balloon to jerk, dislodging Maud. In front of nearly a thousand people, Maud fell two hundred feet to her death. She died instantly, her neck broken and her body badly mangled.

Maud Broadwick was buried in nearby Silver Brook Cemetery. Her tomb, in the Hollywood section of the cemetery, sits alone under a tree, surrounded by plots filled with families.

When she was buried, Charles Broadwick had not yet let her family know that she was dead. Charles, it is said, married the circus's bearded lady just three weeks after her death. Despite the situation surrounding Maud's death, no one blamed Charles for the incident. It was either suicide, they said, or a tragic accident.

Charles continued as an aeronaut with a succession of "Mrs. Broadwicks." But acts like his were already beginning to be outdated. According to the nonfiction book about Anderson's oldest cemetery, *Old Silver Brook Cemetery*, he went on to find another partner, Georgia "Tiny" Jacobs. Tiny stood only four and a half feet tall and weighed eighty-five pounds. She was billed variously as either his wife or his daughter.

In 1908, the fifteen-year-old single mother convinced Broadwick to let her take over Maud's act. Later, as the act became less attractive to customers, she became Broadwick's parachutist from his biplane. In their new act, Tiny, dressed in a doll costume, would drop from a door beneath her seat and parachute to the ground.

In fact, Broadwick is credited with inventions that shaped the parachute as we know it now. When Maud used the parachute, it was released and then, after a short fall, opened, and she floated to safety. But it was hazardous. She was hanging off of a trapeze under a balloon. Any stray gust or breeze could pick her up and throw her into nearby trees or a building.

After Maud's death in 1905, Charles Broadwick invented a new way to release his parachute. Strapped to the back, the invention allowed the parachute to be put into a pack. Once the parachutist jumped, the parachute,

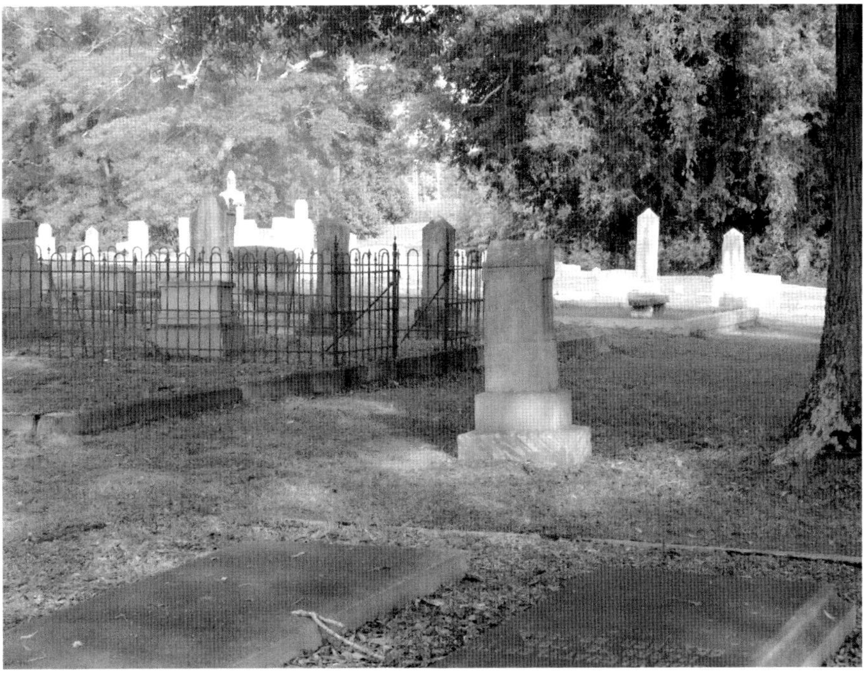

Maud Broadwick's tombstone in Silverbrook Cemetery, Anderson. *Author's collection.*

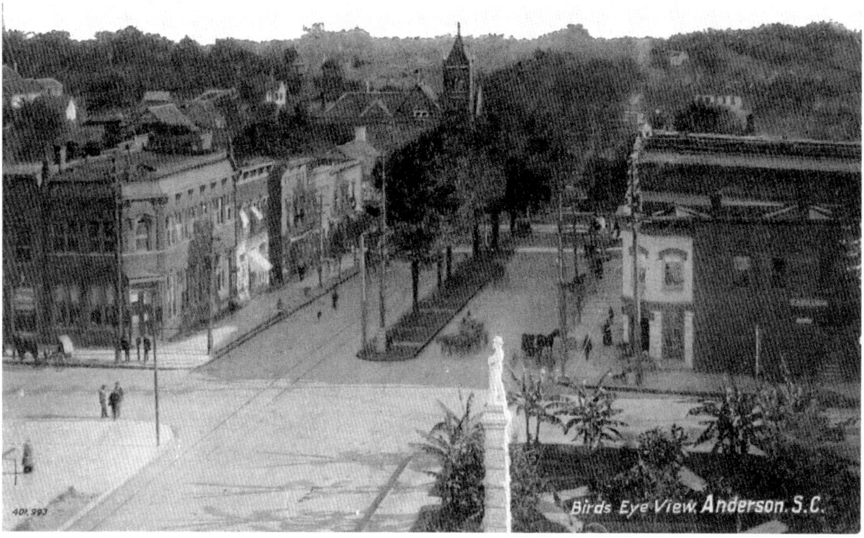

A postcard of downtown Anderson, circa 1910. *Courtesy of South Caroliniana Library, University of South Carolina, Columbia, South Carolina.*

attached to the balloon, would deploy when the static line to it grew taut. That same system is used today to release parachutes.

Broadwick's not-so-successful inventions included a trapdoor parachute for airplanes and a large parachute for a plane itself. The latter was discarded when, during a demonstration, it wrapped around the plane it was intended to save. The pilot, unable to control the plane, felt it dropping rapidly and deployed his own personal parachute. He landed safely on the ground, only narrowly avoiding being hit by the crashing plane.

Georgia Jacobs's life was plagued by parachute disasters and near-disasters. She became famous for her stunts and her demonstration of Broadwick's static cord.

During once such act in 1912, Broadwick and Jacobs showed the audience their jump from a hot-air balloon, to much commotion and intrigue from the crowd. After watching the drop, Glenn Curtiss, an aviation expert, disapproved of the move. "It's much safer for an operator to remain in his seat," he told a reporter, instructing him that he told his pupils to never jump in an emergency.

Later, when Broadwick and Jacobs were demonstrating how well his pack worked when jumping out of an airplane in front of members of Congress, officials from the U.S. Army and some pilots, Tiny jumped three times from the plane. In this demonstration, Tiny exited the plane through a trapdoor, and the static line for the parachute was attached to the plane, deploying her parachute when she fell out the trapdoor. On the fourth jump, however, something went wrong. The cord got tangled in the plane's tail and didn't release the parachute.

Hanging under a moving airplane, Tiny's body was forced against the belly of the plane. Unable to get back into the aircraft, all she could do was save herself by cutting the cord that held her and her parachute to the plane. Even though she was falling toward the earth, somehow, Tiny managed to pull the static line and release the parachute. It was a record for parachuting. Tiny was the first person to successfully parachute from an airplane. In addition, she was the first person to release a parachute by hand and to make a free-fall descent. She was also the first person to make a jump using a parachute over water.

In 1922, Jacobs retired from jumping, after making more than 1,100 jumps, to marry.

Jacobs died in 1978 and was buried in Sunset Gardens in Henderson, North Carolina. In February 2006, Vance County, North Carolina commissioners named part of the Henderson Outer Loop Highway after Jacobs. Broadwick Street in Rancho Dominguez, California, is also named for her.

Broadwick's third wife, Ethel Knutsen, was also known in the circuit as "Tiny." The couple had just settled in San Francisco when they were involved in another parachute accident. In February 1920, Ethel was testing a new parachute design at Marina Airfield when her suspension lines tangled and she fell to her death.

After Ethel's death, Broadwick withdrew from public life, but he continued to work on his parachute designs. Between 1920 and 1940, he continued his work as an inventor. Three of his designs were for parachutes for whole planes.

His designs—for military, commercial and recreational use—are the basis for the parachutes that we still use today and were pioneered by Maud Broadwick in their act.

12

Amelia Earhart Lands in Anderson

In Depression-era South Carolina, the atmosphere was grim. Jobs were scarce. Farms were producing as much as they could for a public who couldn't afford to buy. So, when a certified celebrity dropped in, it was big news.

On November 14, 1931, Amelia Earhart, otherwise known as "Lady Lindy" and the "Queen of the Air," stopped by Anderson in her Pitcairn PCA-2 Autogiro. Landing on the highest spot in Anderson County, near where the Anderson County Civic Center stands within the Anderson Sports and Entertainment Complex today, Earhart stopped long enough to shake a few hands, fuel up and hand out some Beech-Nut chewing gum, which she was promoting.

Before development, before tourists and before the civic center, Anderson County was relatively flat. A hill rose just west of the city seat. It was there, at the highest spot in the county, that the county government placed the airport, such as it was.

No more than a landing strip and a field for emergency landings, really, the airport had been put into the area some three years earlier to accommodate flights in and out of the county, as well as hot-air balloon traffic. But, certainly, the airport had hosted no dignitaries as big as Amelia Earhart. She was by that time an international celebrity. Just a few years earlier, she had gained worldwide fame for record-setting flying exploits. But just a little over ten years before her arrival in Anderson, Earhart was merely a girl with a passion for flying.

Earhart was born in Atchison, Kansas, on July 24, 1897. The daughter of a railroad attorney, she spent her childhood all over Iowa and Kansas with her sister Grace. The two were nicknamed "Meeley" or "Millie" (for Amelia) and "Pidge." The two were brought up unconventionally, owing mostly to Earhart's mother's opinion that she didn't want to raise "nice little girls." Earhart wore "bloomers" from an early age, much to the chagrin of her maternal grandmother and the other girls in her neighborhood.

At nineteen, Earhart attended Ogontz School near Philadelphia, Pennsylvania, a junior college, but she never graduated. She left two years later and enrolled in a Red Cross first-aid course, enlisting as a nurse's aide at Spadina Military Hospital in Toronto, Canada. Among her duties were tending to wounded soldiers during World War I, preparing food in the kitchen for patients with special diets and handing out prescribed medicine in the hospital's dispensary.

Later, Earhart enrolled as a pre-medical student at Columbia University in New York. Not too soon after, though, her parents insisted that she move to California, where they then lived.

Earhart learned to fly in California, taking up aviation first as a hobby. It wasn't an easy task, but it was one she knew she had to do. "By the time I had got to two or three hundred feet off the ground, I knew I had to fly," she said at the time.

After the initial ten-minute flight, she immediately became determined to learn to fly. She worked as a photographer, a truck driver and a stenographer at the local telephone company in order to save up $1,000 for flying lessons. Her first lesson was on January 3, 1921. In order to get to the airfield, Earhart had to take a bus to the end of the line and walk four miles to the airport.

Earhart's mother provided part of the money for her lessons, given by Anita Snook, a pioneer aviator of the day. Six months later, Earhart purchased a secondhand bright yellow Kinner Airster biplane that she nicknamed "The Canary." On October 22, 1922, Earhart flew the Airster to an altitude of fourteen thousand feet, setting a world record for female pilots. On May 15, 1923, Earhart earned her pilot's license from the Federation Aeronautique Internationale—only the sixteenth woman to be awarded a license at the time.

When Earhart's parents divorced, she moved to Medford, Massachusetts, where she was employed as a social worker. But her love of aviation remained. Earhart joined the American Aeronautical Society's Boston chapter, eventually becoming its vice-president, and flew the first official flight out of Dennison Airport in Quincy, Massachusetts. Earhart also worked as a sales representative for Kinner aircraft in the Boston area and wrote local newspaper columns promoting flying. Her celebrity in the Boston area grew.

While there, she was selected by George Palmer Putnam to be the first female passenger on a transatlantic flight. Earhart was to accompany pilot Wilmer Stultz and copilot/mechanic Louis Gordon, as well as keep the flight log.

Putnam, a publisher, had already put out several books written by Charles Lindbergh, and he immediately saw Amelia Earhart's story as a bestseller for his publishing house. Already, her bravery aboard the trimotor plane *Friendship* on its transatlantic trip was being heralded around the world. When the flight was finished, Earhart penned *20 Hrs. 40 Min.: Our Flight in the* Friendship. In interviews, she said she didn't pilot the plane but was just along for the ride. "Stultz did all the flying—had to. I was just baggage, like a sack of potatoes," she said. "Maybe someday I'll try it alone."

In England, a rousing crowd met the threesome. When they returned to New York, they were greeted with a ticker-tape parade and a reception at the White House with President Calvin Coolidge.

As Earhart's celebrity grew, so did Putnam's marketing of her and her book. First, he launched a multicity lecture and book-signing tour. Then, he organized several endorsement deals for Earhart, including luggage, Lucky Strike cigarettes, women's clothing and sportswear.

Her celebrity reached Beech-Nut Packing Company, which was looking for a promotional effort to market its gum. The company decided to have Earhart fly around the country, stopping in towns along the way to promote the gum. In a deal brokered by Putnam, Beech-Nut partnered with Pitcairn to provide Earhart with a plane to fly cross-country. Beech-Nut offered Earhart the use of its Pitcairn PCA-2 Autogiro—which it had ordered prior to the deal being made—on the condition that she fly it coast to coast with the company logo on the plane's side and promote the company's chewing gum. But the plane Beech-Nut ordered would have been the thirteenth produced by the company. Superstitious about such things, Earhart requested a lower production number. Pitcairn promptly gave Beech-Nut and Earhart model number 12.

After a single fifteen- to twenty-minute flying lesson on the autogiro—a plane-helicopter hybrid that used a propeller for forward motion and a unmotorized, freely rotating rotor for lift—she was ready to go. On December 19, 1930, Earhart soloed on the craft at Pitcairn Aviation field in Willow Grove, Pennsylvania, becoming the first woman autogiro pilot and starting her promotional tour.

In the summer of 1931, Earhart traveled across the country, hitting seventy-six communities in twenty-six days. Her stops included Abilene, Texas; Troy, Nevada; Cheyenne, Wyoming; and Glendale, California. After her tour, she became the first woman to fly the autogiro on a transcontinental trip and back. Her attempt at being the first person to fly transcontinental was thwarted by Lieutenant John Miller, who flew out of Willow Grove, Pennsylvania, a few days ahead of Earhart in his lucky number 13 autogiro to little fanfare, beating Earhart by eight days.

After the first promotional tour, Earhart continued to fly for Beech-Nut through the end of 1931. Among the stops was the Upstate. Landing in Anderson, Earhart was met by a welcoming committee: Bonner Kidd, Mr. and Mrs. J.H. Mitchell, Mayor G.T. McGregor, Dr. and Mrs. F.D. Suggs, Peter Thornton, Lou Sullivan, Tom Speer and Bill Garrison.

In total, more than one thousand people gathered to see the lady of the skies. The welcoming committee insisted that Earhart tour Anderson. Soon, the entourage turned into an impromptu parade as well-wishers lined the streets, waiting to get a glimpse of America's high-flying sweetheart. Later,

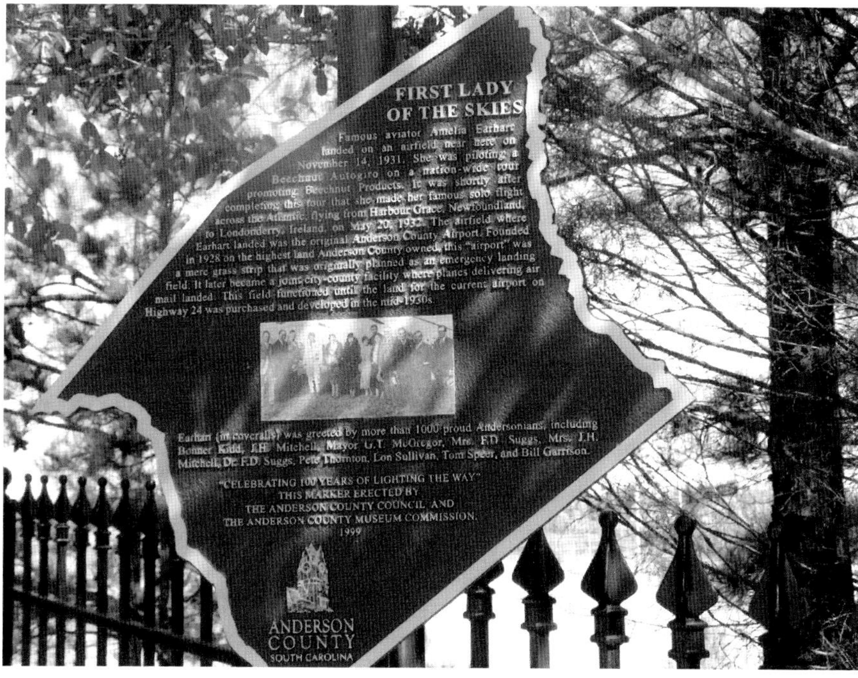

Amelia Earhart's Anderson stop marker, near the Anderson Sports and Entertainment Complex in Anderson. *Author's collection.*

during a tour of Gossett Mills, textile workers presented Earhart with some cloth made at one of the mills.

But as the day grew long, Earhart had to depart. A weekend engagement in Greenville, for the city's centennial celebration, meant it was time to leave. She spent the weekend of November 12–14 in Greenville, including lunch at the Poinsett Hotel and demonstration flights at Greenville's downtown airport, the Greenville Municipal Airport.

One article read: "Miss Amelia Earhart set the first autogiro ever to stop in Greenville down at the local flying field yesterday afternoon as approximately 4,000 persons looked on. She brought the awkward-looking windmill ship down to earth almost vertically….The world-known Miss Earhart, first woman to fly the stormy Atlantic, is flying the autogiro along a route of Southern cities for the Beech Nut Products concern….She will speak at a Dutch luncheon at the Poinsett hotel."

Despite the brief visit, Anderson left an impression on Earhart, one that left her with a longing to come back and visit the kind people who had welcomed her with open arms. "I will do my best to come back to Anderson sometime and when you are in New York come around to see me—I mean that too," she said, according to the *Anderson Daily Mail*. "The welcome here has pleased me more than in any other city on my tour."

13

Vim Herb

Many older Anderson residents will remember starting the school year with a taste of medicine—the elixir of Vim Herb.

Through the 1930s and '40s, Vim Herb was what you took to keep yourself regular and rested. Advertised as relief from headaches, stomach illnesses cause by "faulty elimination" or "biliousness" (otherwise known as nausea or vomiting), it was a staple in some homes in Anderson and throughout the Southeast.

"Patent medicines" were common during the nineteenth and early twentieth centuries. They claimed to be patented formulas for curing everything from the common cold to venereal diseases. Usually, these medicines were in the form of liquids and were made up of a combination of herbs usually mixed with alcohol.

The high levels of alcohol were astounding. But because there wasn't a Food and Drug Administration at the time, there was no way to know how much alcohol was in them. Since their ingredients were often kept secret, they began to be referred to as "quack" medicines. In fact, some had very high levels of alcohol. Lydia Pinkham's Women's Tonic had a 19 percent alcohol content, while Dr. Kilmer's Swamp Root was 12 percent alcohol. Hostetter's Bitters had an amazing level of 32 percent alcohol, making it 64 proof, nearly as high in alcohol as some liquors of the day. To give you an idea, beer is generally between 4 and 20 percent alcohol, while Ouzo is 37.5 percent alcohol and rum ranges anywhere between 35 and 70 percent, the average being 40 percent.

In some cases, the medicines included things like opiates, morphine or cocaine. To make matters worse, the tonics were often prescribed to children, sometimes resulting in horrible outcomes. The medicines were known for giving users a high that made the patent medicines extremely popular among women, who wouldn't be caught dead drinking or doing drugs in public. Behind closed doors, they could take their restoratives and feel better—in more ways than one.

Although many of the tonics and patent medicines were only a ruse, some legitimate medicines that we use today evolved from them. Listerine, started in 1879, promised better oral hygiene, while Bayer Aspirin in 1899 promised headache relief. Phillip's Milk of Magnesia promised to move bowels in 1880, as did Ex-Lax in 1905, and Richardson's Croup and Pneumonia Cure Salve in the 1890s promised to relieve cold symptoms. We now call Richardson's cure Vicks VapoRub.

A number of other products that were thought to have medicinal properties were once marketed as patent medicines. The ingredients may have changed some, but they are still for sale at your local drugstore. Among them are 7 Up, Coca-Cola, Angostura Bitters and tonic water. And who among us hasn't had 7 Up and crackers when feeling nauseated?

Vim Herb, developed after these patent medicines, was part of the cultural phenomenon that relied on those types of "cures." It was a successful constipation cure for more than forty years. Created by Anderson native Alton P. "Doc" Durham, the medicine was advertised in newspapers and on radio shows throughout the South.

Coming in at 15 percent alcohol, the medicine included a mix of stomach bitters and other herbs and roots, including nux vomica, the berries and toxic seeds of the "strychnine tree." The tree originates in India and Asia, and the berries and seeds are often used as a homeopathic treatment for symptoms of overeating and overdrinking. The drug affects the brain and causes muscle contractions. Today, according to WebMD, the use of nux vomica is discouraged, because it can build up strychnine in the body and lead to convulsions and even death.

Vim Herb was sold in drugstores throughout Anderson County. At the time, customers could tell if a drugstore sold the tonic by the big yellow thermometer pasted on the window. A copy of the thermometer is on display at the Anderson County Museum.

Doc Durham began to sell the tonic at 119 West Benson Street. By 1941, the tonic had become so popular that the production moved to a store at the corner of South Main and Franklin Streets. Although the building is

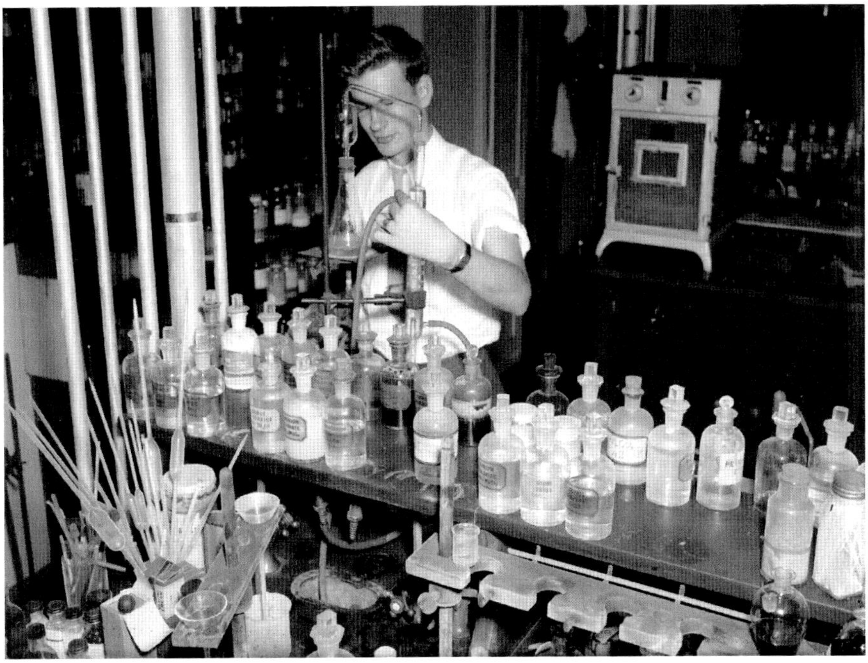

A chemist with the Department of Agriculture tests tonics for alcohol in 1914. *National Archives.*

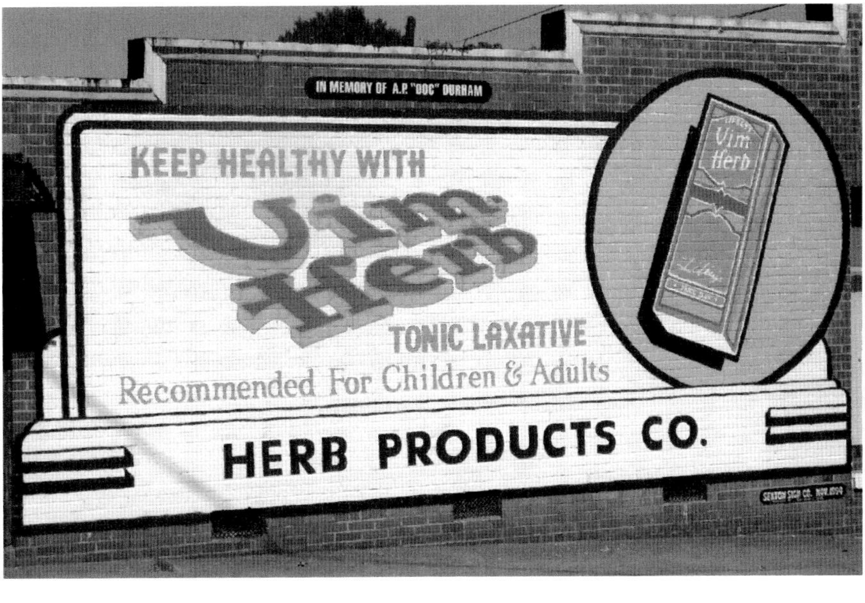

South Main Street, advertisement for Vim Herb. *Author's collection.*

now empty, a painting of the Vim Herb logo remains on the side of the structure, commemorating one of Anderson's most prominent businessmen of the 1940s and '50s.

Finding out how people felt about the drug wasn't difficult. Testimonials showed up in newspapers all over South and North Carolina. With personal endorsements from everyday people, the ads proclaimed that the suffering of various symptoms could be cleared up by using Vim Herb. "Vim Herb is an honest medicine, honestly advertised and a medicine that really gives honest results," one headline reads. "For some time, I had been bothered with headaches. I had no appetite, was weak and didn't feel like doing anything. My system was in run down condition caused by constipation. I tried several kinds of medicines over a period of four years, but I can truthfully say that Vim Herb has helped me more than anything....I have gained weight and eat heartily now that Vim Herb has relieved my system of that constipated condition."

Durham started his career while a teenager, working in pharmacies during World War I. He began looking into herbal medicines. Later, he worked as a traveling salesman at the Herb Juice Medicine Company in Jackson, Tennessee. The company sent Durham to meet with George Washington Carver, who had an herbal formula used to treat tuberculosis.

After training with Carver, Durham returned to Tennessee and worked with B.J. Lifsey to create the Herb Products Medicine Company. Durham was charged with overseeing operations in North and South Carolina. It was then that he made Anderson his home.

Lifsey died in 1938, and Durham took over the production of Lifsey's Vim Herb from the Lifsey family. Sold in five states across the Southeast, it was most widely known and used in the Anderson area.

It wasn't unusual to hear the Vim Herb jingle on WAIM radio several times a day or to pick up a newspaper with a front-page testimonial of the medicine's success.

As late at 2008, a local Andersonian made a YouTube video singing the Vim Herb jingle in front of the Vim Herb wall for his eightieth birthday. Obviously, the catchy song has lingered in some Andersonians' heads:

> *When you're feeling weak and helpless and you don't know what to do / and the world seems out to get you and your nerves go back on you / Then it's time to cleanse your system of the poisons gathered there / A small dose taken in the morning, another noon and night / You'll feel so well, you'll want to yell / Vim Herb has made me right!*

On the radio, Vim Herb was hawked by "Ramblin' Tommy" Scott. The Toccoa native first joined Doc Chamberlain's Medicine Show and then moved on to the radio, getting his first gig on WTFL in Athens, Georgia. Scott sold Vim Herb on the air. Later, when Chamberlain retired, he gave his patent medicines to Scott, who continued to sell Vim Herb.

Doc Durham was also known for his charity work in the Anderson area, especially selling war bonds and holding paper drives during World War II. He served as the Anderson Area Chamber of Commerce's president, was director of the Anderson County Tuberculosis Association, president of the Anderson Fair Association and director of the T.L. Hanna Yellow Jackets Booster Club. He also served on the boards of the Salvation Army and Anderson Memorial Hospital, now AnMed Health.

Durham recruited the Anderson Rebels, a minor league baseball team, to the city.

An article in the Anderson *Daily Mail* referred to Durham as the "unofficial public relations representative" of Anderson for all of his work in the community. The product he created wasn't without its problems, however. In 1937, the United States attorney for the Northern District of Georgia seized nearly one hundred bottles of Vim Herb in response to a report from the secretary of agriculture. The report claimed that the bottles were misbranded in violation of the Food and Drug Act.

The complaint against Vim Herb was that it didn't do what was promised. According to the complaint, the medicine's packaging indicated that it would cure:

> *constipation; stomach, liver and kidney disorders and all impoverished or changed conditions of the system; and disorders of the blood; and would be effective to cleanse the system and restore ills caused by attending constipation including fullness after meals, dizziness, biliousness [nausea] and coated tongue; effective to restore vim, vigor, vitality and health; effective to restore perfect health; would be effective in purifying, strengthening, upbuilding and revitalizing the system; effective in restoring health, destroying poisons that cause sickness; effective supplying perfect heath and vigorous vitality; effective as a medicine for the entire system and would afford relief from all stomach, liver, kidney and bowel difficulties.*

When no one showed up at the hearing in Atlanta on March 1, the medicine was condemned and the bottles destroyed.

Durham's business didn't suffer from the findings, however. He went on to sell Vim Herb well into the 1970s. When the business closed, Durham sold his Anderson home and retired to a farm in Abbeville to raise cattle and horses. He died there in 1984 at the age of eighty.

14

Anderson County's Textile Mill Strikes

Following the Civil War, southern states looked to manufacturing to ease the burden of economic turmoil.

Starting in the 1870s, many southern states turned to textile manufacturing to stimulate their economies. Based on the success of mills in the North, southern states made the most of their abundance of cheap labor and cotton (their two biggest resources), as well as their more temperate climate and lower taxes.

With the rallying cry of "Bring the cotton mills to the cotton fields," states across the South invested heavily in creating a textile revolution. As northern investors poured money into the mills, they also created mill villages—housing complexes where workers lived with their families.

The idea behind mill villages was to encourage loyalty in workers. Rent was paid to the company, usually based on how many people living in the building worked at the mill. Often, the mill would set the rent at from fifty cents to a dollar per room and require a certain number of workers per house, such as one person per bedroom, or two people per three bedrooms. Entire families sometimes worked at the mill.

Mill owners thought that workers would be appreciative of their generosity and largesse. In reality, though, mill work was often just a step above poverty and paid so poorly that workers would become stuck in an endless loop of debt to the company.

The typical mill employee worked a six-day week, with only Sundays off. Work started at 6:00 a.m. and stopped around 6:00 p.m. In the 1880s,

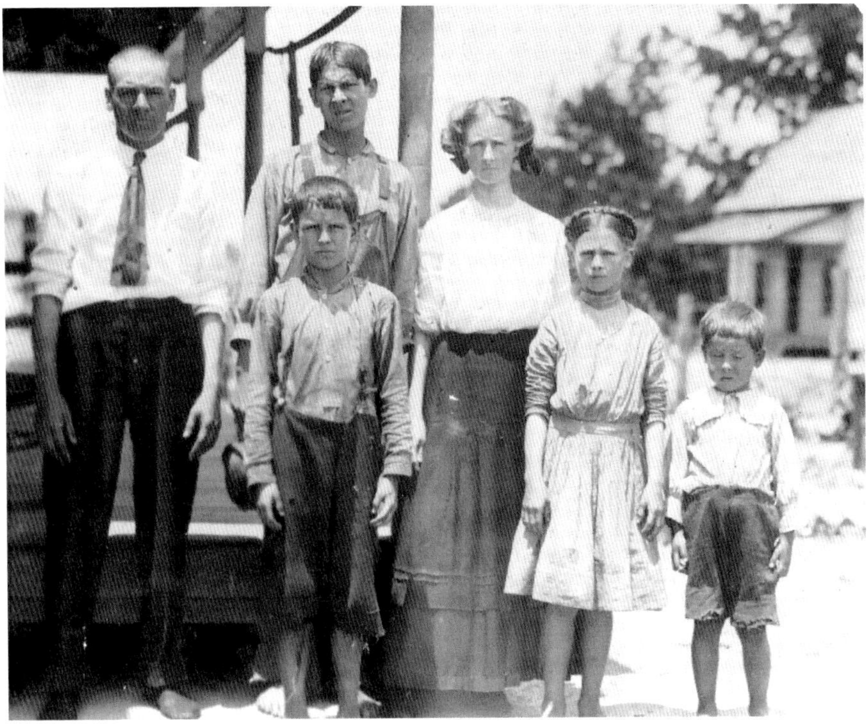

Belton Mill family, circa 1920. *National Archives.*

workers made an average of $0.12 a day. Men made the most in the mills. Women made one-half to two-thirds of what men made; children made even less than that. And supervisors made sure that employees were working and not lollygagging. Women often complained that they didn't have time to go to the restroom before being accused of dillydallying. The average family made just $1,000.00 a year at a mill. And most of that went back to the company.

Mill villages spun out from mills like webs. Textile companies would build houses, churches, stores and schools for workers to live in. Isolated from towns, the mill villages provided everything a worker might need. The employees were essentially caught up in the mill's web. Stores, stocked with inventory paid for by the company, were the only places workers could shop, leaving no competition for prices and workers and their families dependent on the mills.

In the villages, mill superintendents were in charge of managing not only the factory but also the village, standing in for whatever local government the village didn't have. Schools hired single, childless women to be teachers. In some cases, the owners even hired the ministers and instructed them on what to preach, especially on the values of hard work.

Mills offered social clubs and activities to keep workers happy. When workers got frustrated with conditions at the mills, owners brought in leisure and recreational activities. Sewing clubs, garden clubs, flower and fashion shows, cooking schools and baseball teams provided workers with distractions from their hard, daily life.

Protest songs about life in the mills rose up in the 1920s. "Cotton Mill Colic," written by David McCarn in 1926, illustrated the hardships mill workers endured at the hands of the owners in these villages.

Cotton Mill Colic
When you buy clothes on easy terms,
The collector treats you like measly worms;
One dollar down and then, Lord knows,
If you don't make a payment they'll take your clothes.

When you go to bed, you can't sleep,
You owe so much at the end of the week.
No use to collect, they're all that way,
Peckin' at your door till they get your pay.

Chorus:
I'm a-gonna starve, ev'rybody will.
You can't make a livin' at a cotton mill.

When you go to work, you work like the devil,
At the end of the week you're not on the level.
Pay day comes, you pay your rent.
When you get through, you've not got a cent

To buy fat-back meat, and pinto beans
Now and then you get a turnip green.
No use to collect, they're all that way,
You can't get the money to move away.

I'm a-gonna starve, ev'rybody will.
You can't make a livin' at a cotton mill.

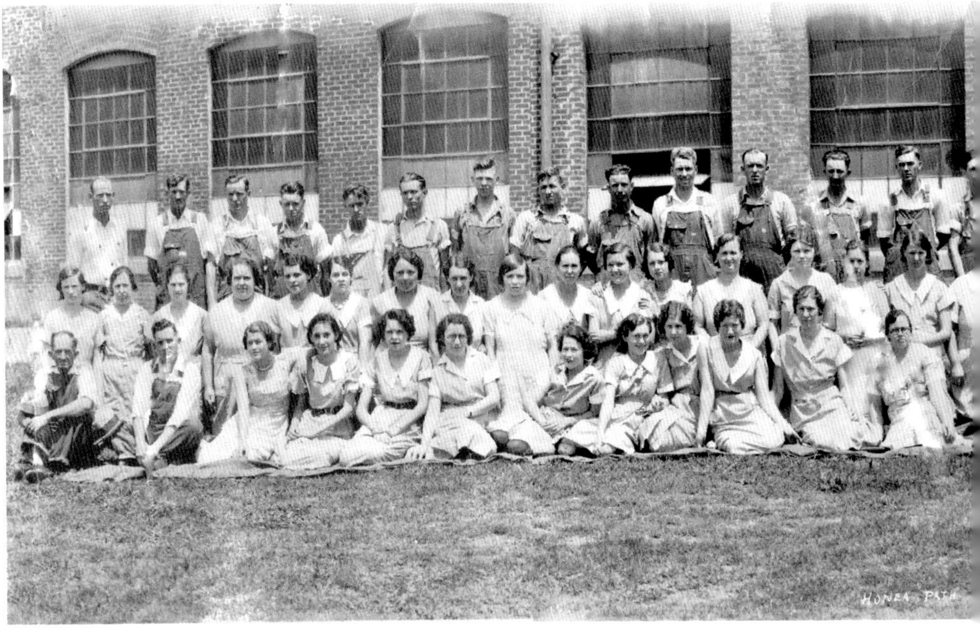

Card deptartment, Chiquola Mill, 1904. *Courtesy Frank Beacham.*

Twelve dollars a week is all I get
How in the heck can I live on that?
I got a wife and fourteen kids,
We all have to sleep on two bedsteads.

Patches on my breeches, holes in my hat,
Isn't had a shave since my wife got fat.
No use to collect, ever' day at noon
Kids get to cryin' in a different tune.

I'm a-gonna starve, ev'rybody will.
You can't make a livin' at a cotton mill.

They run a few days, and then they stand
Just to keep down the workin'man.
We'll never make it, we never will,
As long as we stay in a roundin' mill.

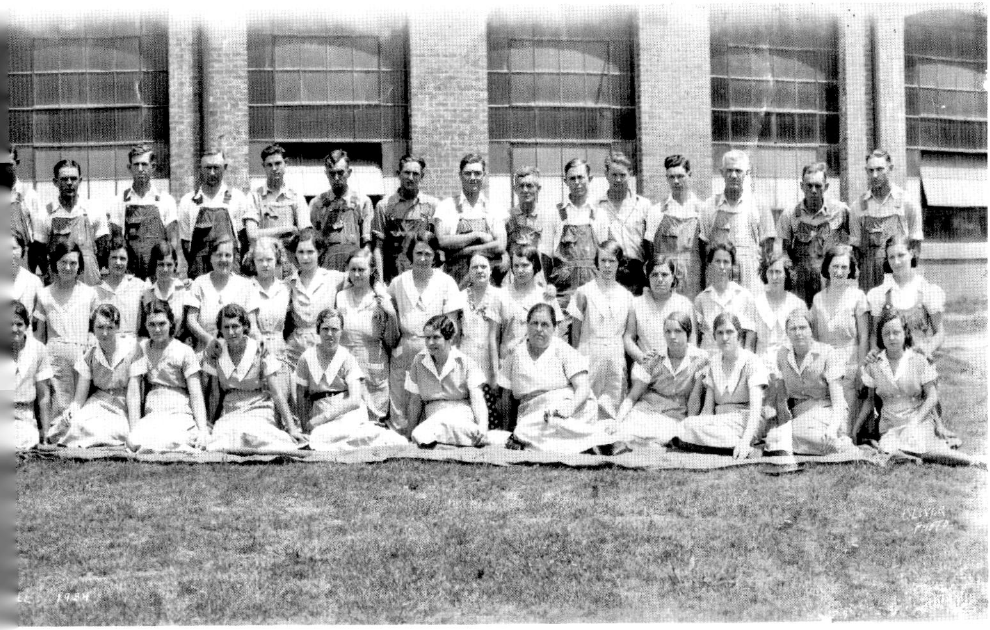

The poor are gettin' poorer, the rich are gettin' rich,
If I don't starve, I'm a son of a gun.
No use to collect, no use to rave,
We'll never rest till we're in our grave.

I'm a-gonna starve, ev'rybody will.
You can't make a livin' at a cotton mill.

For all the problems, though, life in the mill village supported workers emotionally in the years before World War I. Workers made the mill community their family. Sometimes, families would band together to form a sort of extended family, in which all of the families worked together as a unit. Community members gathered together on their one day off to celebrate holidays and weddings.

Women would jump in to help when someone got sick. In an activity called a "pounding," women would bring a pound or two of food to the sick person's home. Other women learned how to use herbal medicine and midwifery to raise their status in the community. Village men provided music—playing the banjo, fiddle or guitar—to boost their own self-worth, both for themselves and in the eyes of their neighbors. These bonds and relationships inside the community brought the workers closer together and created a sense of solidarity.

Little did they know how useful that would be in the years to come.

America's entry into World War I in 1917 meant big changes for the prosperous mill industry. The need for uniforms created demand for cloth, and many mills were awarded government contracts. As workloads increased, however, many of the male workers were drafted into the armed forces, and women left the mills to help on family farms. As a result, the mills saw labor shortages. Mill owners offered higher wages and better homes to attract workers, and some asked the government to excuse their workers from the draft.

Following the war, though, mills faced a number of new challenges. Families struggled with losses, either from military deaths or the influenza epidemic of 1918. As postwar fashions changed—hemlines got shorter and foreign imports of fabric increased, decreasing the demand for fabric—mills faced a surplus of both fabric and employees. Additionally, the invention of machinery to help in the manufacturing process meant too many workers and not enough work.

In order to maintain profits, manufacturers tried to reduce the oversupply by creating industry associations to regulate competition. But the big problem for them was employees. Mill owners needed more work from employees to make them profitable. The solution was called the "stretch-out."

In a stretch-out, mill owners put more mechanical looms under each employee and speeded up production while giving them less time to accomplish their duties. Break times were reduced, piece rates were implemented and the number of supervisors was increased to keep workers from slowing down, talking or leaving work.

By 1929, workers across the country were tired of the stretch-out conditions. Prior to the Great Depression, strikes were happening all over the South. By some accounts, there were more than eighty strikes—non-organized, spontaneous walkouts—in South Carolina in 1929 alone.

As the Great Depression deepened, textile mills in the North started to fold, leaving fewer jobs in the industry. Mill operators laid off workers and increased the amount and pace of work for the employees who remained.

By mid-1933, President Franklin Delano Roosevelt had instituted the National Industrial Recovery Act (NIRA) to help regulate industries, heighten wages and stimulate the economy. But with NIRA governing boards made up of mill owners and operators, the deck remained stacked against the employees. When regulations limited employees to a forty-hour workweek, employers simply required the workers to do in forty hours what they had previously done in a fifty- or sixty-hour week.

In 1934, things came to a head. Employees across the country had filed more than four thousand complaints against their bosses, the mill owners, only one of which was upheld. In South Carolina's Horse Creek Valley, employees struck to get employers to live up to the NIRA codes. Strikers faced special deputies, highway patrolmen and a machine-gun unit of the National Guard sent to keep the mills open.

When the NIRA's special board came to oversee the situation, it ignored worker accusations and asked them to return to work. But when workers tried to go back, mill owners not only kept them out of the mills but also kicked them out of their company housing. The result was a work stoppage. Called the General Textile Strike of 1934, it involved union textile workers all across the country walking off the job to protest the working conditions in the mills.

Across South Carolina, however, mills stayed open, even as the zero hour for all work stoppage approached. With the mills open, a "flying squadron," made up of strikers and union sympathizers, made its way to Honea Path. As a rule, flying squadrons were orderly and engaged in activities to encourage mill workers to join in the strikes. South Carolina governor Ibra C. Blackwood called out the National Guard to preserve order. More than seven hundred National Guardsmen were stationed in Greenville. Another six hundred citizens were deputized in the city of Anderson.

On September 6, 1934, when the flying squadron got to Honea Path, it was met by striking workers as well as deputies and excited townsmen. About three hundred union textile workers from Honea Path and Belton surrounded the Chiquola Mill to protest working conditions and wages. The goal was to stop work and make employers and owners pay attention to their complaints.

Instead of getting attention, the demonstrators got knuckle sandwiches. Fistfights broke out around the plant entrance. Then, around 7:45 p.m., non-union workers and the "special deputies" stationed in and around the mill opened fire on the strikers. Shooting into the picket line with pistols and shotguns, the strike busters were determined to end the strike by any means necessary.

Anderson County sheriff W.A. Clamp told the *Anderson Independent* the next day that he felt "lucky to have survived it." "I don't know who shot first," he said at the time. "Bullets kicked up around my feet, and they were shooting pistols, rifles and shotguns. The firing lasted just a couple of minutes and there really wasn't time to do much of anything."

When the dust settled, it was clear that the strikers had suffered the most. The shooting left seven union workers dead and some twenty others wounded. Those killed were the following: Claude Cannon, twenty-seven; Lee Crawford, twenty-six; Thomas Yarbrough, fifty-four; Ira Davis, twenty-six; Maxine Peterson, twenty-seven; C.R. Rucker, thirty-eight; and E.M. "Bill" Knight, age unknown. Some of the dead had been shot as many as ten times.

To this day, no one is sure who gave the order to fire first. Many think it was J.D. Beacham, supervisor at the plant and Honea Path's mayor at the time. According to reports in the *Anderson Independent*, Beacham had quietly sworn in another one hundred "special deputies" in addition to the non-union workers and National Guard officers who had been specifically hired to guard the Chiquola Mill.

Once the fighting started, it was Beacham who supposedly gave the order to non-union workers and deputies to fire on the strikers. Other accounts contend that it was the striking workers who fired first.

Similar strikes happened all over the South. Members of the National Association of Manufacturers issued a statement that the strikes were against national security. "The strikes must be viewed as a direct threat to orderly government," the group said. The group also demonized any federal relief funds to assist those who walked out. "Such a policy is tantamount to government underwriting force instead of preserving the peace," it said.

Governor Blackwood issued a proclamation against flying squadrons. The Chiquola Mill opened again the following Monday, protected by National Guardsmen with machine guns. Within a month, all of the striking workers had returned to work.

While the strike at the national level failed to attract any attention to the plight of the textile worker, the events in Honea Path made a difference. The shooting made national headlines, which made the event a crucial turning point regarding the tide of reform in the textile mills. The incident caught the attention of President Roosevelt and spurred the passage of the National Labor Relations Act, known as the Wagner Act, in 1935 and the Fair Labor Standards Act in 1938.

These two laws reformed labor in America. The Fair Labor Standards Act outlawed child workers under the age of sixteen. Prior to the act, children were allowed to "help" their parents in the mill to augment the family income. The system operated as a form of apprenticeship and served as a major part of the mill's labor system. Other reforms included the establishment of the minimum wage and a better understanding of the forty-hour workweek.

But in Honea Path, no one talked about the incident, which, many decades later, came to be known as the Honea Path Massacre. Whether through fear, intimidation or pride, the Honea Path riots were a specially kept secret in the area for more than two generations. The incident split families and communities, but they stood together in their solidarity to not speak of the event.

In fact, Lois McClain, a spinning-room worker who was injured in the strike, never spoke of it again. Photographed immediately after the strike, McClain was shot in the forearm during the uprising. The bullet was never removed. Her husband, Cowan, also worked at the mill, but he was uninjured. "Granny Lois," as she was later called, went on to work at the mill until she was in her seventies. The mother of five children, she also volunteered in the mill village as a seamstress, cook and midwife to the workers.

Years after the riots, another worker, Tom Stalcup, admitted that he had been the one who had shot her, and he asked for her forgiveness. She forgave him immediately. Stalcup went on to be a Sunday school teacher, eventually teaching the Gospel to one of McClain's daughters.

According to her family, neither Lois nor her husband ever spoke of the uprising to any of their children. When she died in 1993, with the bullet still lodged in her forearm, Lois's secrets and the story of how she was injured died with her.

It wasn't until the 1990s, with the release of the movie *Uprising of '34* by George Stoney and other independent filmmakers, that some people in the area even learned that the riots had happened. Frank Beacham, the grandson of J.D. Beacham, discovered the story and later wrote a book about the events, *Whitewash: A Southern Journey Through Music, Mayhem and Murder*. Angered by the actions of his grandfather, Frank was instrumental in raising a monument to the slain strikers and those wounded in the riots.

The monument stands in Honea Path today, just a mile from where the Chiquola Mill once stood. Dedicated in May 1995, the monument remembers the seven who "died for the rights of the working man."

PELZER TEXTILE MILL STRIKES

Honea Path wasn't the only town in Anderson County to see violent uprisings at its textile mills.

Twenty-four miles to the north, at the Pelzer Manufacturing Company, union members didn't want to strike.

The Pelzer Manufacturing Company was composed of four plants, three of which—Plants 1, 2 and 3—stood along the southern end of Pelzer on the banks of the Saluda River. The fourth, Plant 4, was on the northern edge of town, up on a hill, about a mile from the other three.

When the national unions called for sympathy strikes to bring attention to difficulties cotton textile workers were having in other areas, the Pelzer union voted not to strike. Life was good for mill workers in Pelzer. The company generally supported its workers and was fair. The pay and hours were considered good for the region. And the supervisors supported workers joining the union. The Pelzer union members had no beef with the way they were treated.

Regardless of their vote, however, flying squadrons from Spartanburg came to the Pelzer plants and shut them down. At the time, the Pelzer union was able to count about 90 percent of the millworkers as members. But the plant shutdown so angered some of the workers, who felt the union was working against their wishes, that they walked out of the union.

Unlike at Honea Path, the Pelzer strike was peaceful, and both union and company workers cooperated. Some even reported that the strike was treated more like a vacation than a walkout—"[drinking] cokes and coffee out on the grass and [having] a grand time."

But the men who had walked out were not to be mollified. Led by George McCall, George Herbert and Jim Westmoreland, the former union members formed their own organization, the Good Will Club. The group met in the YMCA across from Plant 1. While they supported the company, Pelzer Manufacturing Company superintendent J.F. Blackmon said the company never had a hand in establishing the club.

As time wore on, the union lost favor among the company and its employees. Union members started to feel that the Good Will Club was being used by management to put a wedge between union members. Eventually, when union men would be let go, union members started to think that they were being discriminated against. With its membership down to only 40 percent of the workers at the plant, the union had lost its strength through numbers, and the company refused to bargain with it.

In fact, the company refused to let the union meet on company property, leaving union members to meet in open fields or near railroad tracks.

In the spring of 1935, union members asked Paul Ross to be president of the union. His directives were to bring back union membership and reestablish bargaining power with company management. It was a time before the Wagner Act, and unions operated without legal protections—and this union operated without any facility in which to meet or organize.

Ross had another issue to deal with almost immediately, however. Spreading through the Pelzer Manufacturing workforce was the feeling that there should be a strike to show management that the union was a force to be reckoned with. Union leaders felt the idea had been planted in workers' heads by the company in order to further damage the union. Company leaders felt the idea had been planted by the national union representatives.

Still, a meeting for the union was called to vote on whether or not to strike. That night, in the woods, the union's usual meeting place, the group chose by voice vote. The vote carried. When the next union man was fired, the union members would strike. But Ross and other union leaders felt that the vote was swayed by agitators and non-union members from neighboring towns looking to make trouble for the union men. With no official tabulation or accurate count, there was no way to tell who voted, or how. Even though local union leaders advised against it, the die was cast. "We were sitting on a powder keg that I was hoping wouldn't explode," Ross later told researcher Rich Otter.

Before anyone could strike, the Wagner Act passed. With it came protections for union members through collective bargaining, the right to meet and protection from discrimination.

It wasn't long, though, before a union member was on the chopping block. On Friday, July 12, "Unck" Smith got wind that his hours were being cut. He returned to work with a knife. When he drew it on his boss and tried to replace another worker, he was forcibly removed from the plant. The strikers were prepared, though. After a short meeting, they decided they'd strike after the second shift on Monday, July 15.

Just enough men struck to slow work but not to shut down the plant. And while the strikers were quiet and peaceful, by Monday night, William Johnston, the Anderson-based brother of Governor Olin Johnston, had arrived on the scene to check out the situation. According to Governor Johnston, members of the Good Will Club and the Pelzer Manufacturing Company had called Columbia, asking officials to send in protection for non-striking workers. And according to Superintendent Blackmon, company law enforcement officer Constable J.L. Cole had been shot at.

For his part, William Johnston spoke with union members, non-union members and company officials before deciding the that non-striking workers needed protection. On Thursday, the 118th Infantry of the National Guard arrived from Greenville and imposed martial law in Pelzer.

For six days, the strike was quiet—and ineffective.

When Ross got nowhere with Blackmon and other company officials, union members traveled to Columbia to plead with Governor Johnston for help. Johnston, in turn, called Blackmon and arranged a meeting for the two sides to come to an agreement. For days, the negotiations continued as strikers remained quiet. But in the mill villages, the families of twelve strikers were facing eviction proceedings.

On Sunday, the men met at Blackmon's summer home. Management agreed to consider the cases of alleged discrimination and would allow strikers to return to their posts, provided the jobs weren't already filled. The only exceptions were the strikers who had been seen on the picket lines armed or who had turned off machines that weren't theirs. But, company leaders said, union members shouldn't expect too much to come out of the discrimination cases.

With their backs against the wall, union officials met with their members and announced their decision: they were going to reject the offer. They felt the exceptions to the agreements were nothing more than a way for the company to punish union leaders and other union members.

For another week, union members struck. While the leaders continued to press for a meeting with company officials, no meetings took place. As the strike wore on, even attempts by Governor Johnston proved fruitless. For union members, it meant another week without pay. And while the American Federation of Labor had promised to help the workers, no money had yet arrived. Union leaders visited other cities, passing the hat and begging for help, and striking workers signed on to the federal government's Works Progress Administration to support themselves and their families.

By August 14, nearly a month after the strike had begun, the state government called company officials and union workers to Columbia. The state wanted to see an end to the strike. Mostly, the state was tired of paying the $750 a day to protect the strikers. The state issued a proposal to settle the dispute through arbitration. Union officials agreed. Company officials refused. So, the strike continued.

On Monday, August 19, the company moved to evict the families of thirty strikers. Again, the state tried to resolve the conflict, but again, after considering the offer for another five days, the company refused to agree to the state's proposal to settle the dispute through arbitration. Governor Johnston, in response, ordered the National Guard troops home. Johnston said he had done everything he could but if management refused to come to the table, he couldn't continue to protect it, especially with not so much as a fistfight occurring between the strikers and non-strikers.

With the military gone, strikers surrounded the four plants. Still, throughout the weekend, the strike remained quiet. But tensions were building. By Sunday night, meetings in advance of the coming workweek were happening all over Pelzer. Strikers and non-strikers alike were carrying guns. Union men held their places on the picket line, while non-union men planned what to do if strikers attacked them. It wasn't long before those on the picket line heard noises.

One of the strikers heard noises coming from the railroad tracks that ran beside Plant 4. Rumors started that non-union men were massing outside of the plant and planning to enter it through the boiler room. In retaliation, a small group of strikers grabbed a stick of dynamite, ripping the wrapper off and pouring the powder into a small tin. Within moments, the men had created a small bomb intended to frighten but not injure. They lit it and flung it toward the non-striking millworkers. The bomb landed within one hundred yards of where they were gathered and sent men fleeing in all directions. Union men ran down the hill and collected the weapons and ammunition the fleeing men had left behind.

After that, the area around Plant 4 was quiet. But a mile away, Plant 1 was active. Non-striking workers had entered the plant and could be seen walking in front of windows. Rumors flew up and down the picket line. Some alleged that the men had snuck in the back of the plant while picketers were held at gunpoint, while others swore that those inside the plant had been let in by company guards. And while some held that the men inside the plant should be removed before someone got hurt, others looked up from the picket lines to see the glimmering steel of the rifles of the men inside.

Throughout the night, reports of shooting echoed down the streets of Pelzer as strikers and non-strikers alike shot others roaming the streets. Superintendent Blackmon and Anderson County's Sheriff Clamp called Governor Johnston again, pleading for more military help. But the governor refused, saying he couldn't protect some of the workers while others remained out of employment.

Blackmon closed the four plants. But no one told the workers. When the work bell rang, employees walked down the hill to their plants. Striking workers lined the streets. Some workers returned home. Others stayed to watch what was happening. Still others had come prepared and clutched tightly to their guns.

According to union president Ross, one of the plant superintendents, a Mr. Edwards, came down the street headed to Plant 4 in his car, laughing and greeting the picketers. When picketers asked if one of the union men could enter the plant with him, he laughed, refused them and ran his car into a line of striking workers. As he barreled over the picket line, someone reacted and threw a brick into the back of his car. That, witnesses said, was when all hell broke loose.

On either side of the conflict, bullets flew. Firing broke out from the plant windows and from the top of the hill. Another group of men circled around the plant and started firing on the striking workers. The picket line broke; those who had held the line opened fire from behind a retaining wall that ran along the road to the plant. Those in the crossfire ran for cover or hid where they stood. Ross saw a woman, Sybil Power, crouching near the gas station that bordered the plant. Running to her, he got her up and led her behind the gas station. A bullet ricocheted off a wall and hit Power in the leg, leaving a large, hand-sized bruise.

Non-striking workers advanced on the union men with guns blazing. Ross tried to move his car but found himself caught in a hail of bullets. Next, a stick of dynamite came rolling down the hill. Ross dove into his car to escape the blast. While it didn't damage the car, it did stop the shooting. The advancing non-striking workers stopped in their tracks and ran back up the hill. Shooting declined to only sporadic bursts now and again.

In the lull, Ross climbed from the car. Near the gas station, he found a young boy who had been shot. He'd been hit in the back of the knee and in his stomach. Ross and another union man decided to break through the line of non-striking workers to get the boy to a hospital. Through another hail of bullets, they drove through the line and delivered the boy to Anderson Memorial Hospital. The boy had been shot thirteen times in the abdomen.

Back at the plant, others weren't faring so well. James Saxton had been shot in the shoulder, and Mrs. Jack Kelly had been shot to death near the railroad. A .45 caliber bullet had ricocheted off the concrete and pierced her neck. The woman's father, B.B. Brown, had been watching the shooting from a nearby bridge. As men carried his daughter by, he ran toward them. As he reached her, she breathed one last time and died in front of him.

An inquest into the shooting resulted in no clear identification of her assailant. While Ross testified that he saw Constable Cole and two other company men shooting, others testified that the shooters had been union men who had shot into the area where the woman had been standing.

The shooting at Plant 1 had lasted less than five minutes, but the shoot-out at Plant 4 had lasted nearly an hour.

As the dust settled, the company and union finally came together to settle the strike. Through arbitration, the company was able to determine who among the strikers should be allowed to return to work, while the union members won the right to air their grievances against the company.

In time, the union left the plant, as did the Good Will Club. Families torn apart by the strike renewed their intimacies, and life in the small town of Pelzer returned to normal. The holding company that owned the mill sold it to another organization within a year, and Superintendent Blackmon stayed on. As times changed, the mill village homes were sold to the millworkers who lived in them, and the company stores were turned over to private owners.

A second casualty of the conflict, Al Burnum, the superintendent of Plant 4, was found dead from a shotgun wound to the head shortly after the strike ended. Many assumed it was suicide.

Unlike the Honea Path riots, the Pelzer strike garnered no national attention. But for the residents of Pelzer, the conflict was a reminder of the freedom to work and organize pitted against the freedom of a company to maintain its business. In the end, both sides lost. But Pelzer, ultimately, won.

15

The Anderson Blitz

Brown's Raid in the summer of 1865 wasn't the only time Anderson was invaded and occupied by military forces.

On the morning of July 11, 1941, an airplane circled downtown Anderson and released thousands of fliers. Anderson was to be attacked that day, the papers told the city's nearly twenty thousand citizens. Resistance would be futile, the fliers said.

And at precisely 7:30 p.m., 450 of the invaders struck. From strategically placed positions, the invaders took over control of public utilities, communications, transportation and military facilities within sixty seconds of starting. As crowds of onlookers, and even some visitors, came downtown to watch, more than 1,300 uniformed soldiers and other subversive elements stormed into the area, meeting at the square and then disbursing in smaller units to the places already seized by invading forces.

Soldiers and "fifth columnists" quickly took over government buildings, television and radio stations, the police station and even the post office. As soldiers took up strategic positions on buildings and around the downtown area to ward off any uprisings or retaliation, others swarmed into government offices and forced officials out into the street at gunpoint.

Fifth columnists are defined as a group of people who undermine a larger group—such as a nation or a besieged city—from within, usually in favor of an enemy group or nation. The fifth columnists in this event, previously masquerading as tourists, helped soldiers take over the press, issuing demands and making proclamations in favor of "Clemsonia."

Soldiers seized the armory. Even hardware stores were prohibited from selling weapons to civilians, in order to prevent retaliation or an uprising. Officials could only watch as they were herded into concentration camps.

The invaders were quick, efficient and prepared. Smoke rose over the streets. Textile mills sounded their whistles to let citizens know that bombing airplanes were on their way. Explosions rocked the city as soldiers pushed citizens aside to show how a blitzkrieg attack should be done.

But that's exactly what it was. All show.

The invasion was an exercise for ROTC students visiting Clemson University. It came at the end of six weeks of training for future infantry officers from colleges and military schools across the South. It was the first time such a large-scale exercise had taken place in a modern city in the United States, according to Colonel W.L. Roberts, the camp director, who conceived of and initiated the exercise.

The mock invasion was designed to show ROTC cadets, officials and others modern European war maneuvers and how easy they were to implement.

For days leading up to the attack, "Clemsonia" placed increasing demands on "Andersonia." Tensions mounted quickly. Suspected members of the fifth column were arrested and detained—their names noted only as "John Doe" when they refused to answer questions. Pistols, belts and weapons of the alleged traitors were seized and news of their detention publicized.

Martial law was ordered, and local officials hurried to send their forces out to protect the town. Local defense forces attempted last-minute maneuvers to stave off the attack, and ultimately, the city officials gave in to Clemsonian demands.

But Clemsonian troops surprised the city and attacked anyway. Smoke pots simulated burning buildings. Airplanes flew overhead. Fireworks stood in for explosions. But the people were real. Members of the ROTC, as well as some actors from the city, were employed to become the fifth column and help destroy Anderson from the inside.

The exercise was meant to recreate as accurately as possible the tactics and methods used by Nazi forces in their invasion of Holland, which had fallen to the Germans on May 10 of the previous year. After five days of fighting, the government of Holland surrendered.

Holland had stayed out of World War I and was considered a safe harbor for Jews in World War II. Many of the Jews attempted to flee the country, but most of those attempts were unsuccessful; the countries bordering Holland were already under German control, and the waters on the

North Sea coastline were patrolled by the Germans. A densely populated country, Holland had more than nine million people in a land area the size of Massachusetts. But the flat land provided little cover for hiding or resistance activities.

At the time of Holland's seizure, an estimated 140,000 Jews lived there. By the war's end, 107,000 had been deported by the Nazis. Only 5,000 managed to survive and return home.

America was at that time an outsider in the war. However, German attacks on U.S. and Allied ships in the Atlantic led President Roosevelt to send Britain fifty World War I destroyers to help the nation defend itself and others. Roosevelt also helped protect Greenland and Iceland so that Britain could defend itself better in the Atlantic.

While the war was far off, the prospect of America entering the conflict was a fear in the hearts of many and the subject of a good deal of the discussion around radios, in barbershops and at dinner tables in the American heartland. For weeks leading up to the invasion of Anderson, city officials and the local newspapers had worked with the camp and its leader to help stage the attack.

Once the real mayor of Anderson was captured, he was forced to give the city over to "General Squarehead," in reality Cadet Ed Glusman, a junior at Louisiana State University.

Since the invading forces had thrown smoke pots at every corner along Main Street and then all along connecting streets east, west and south, the city was covered in a thick white smoke. Rising over the courthouse, the smoke masked the real identity of explosions up and down the city's streets.

After the seizure, the ROTC even issued a newspaper outlining its demands. Among them: seizing all automobiles, hostage-taking, confiscating all money and silverware, the closing of places of entertainment, restricting the use of radios and banning the sale of gasoline.

"Right of Free Speech Withdrawn," the paper read.

> *Communication by mail, Telegraph, Cable, Telephone, Radio, Pigeon and otherwise. A-It is forbidden to send, transmit or knowingly receive by any means of communication whatever any information concerning the ROTC forces. It is forbidden to send, transmit, or knowingly receive by any means whatever any message containing anything hostile, detrimental or disrespectful to the ROTC, its armed forces, their personnel, or the military government. B-All communications, by whatever means transmitted, are subject to censorship. C-The use in any communication by whatever means*

> *transmitted of any language other than ROTC or Andersonian or of a code or other device concealing the true meaning of the message is forbidden.*

The *Anderson Daily Mail* even had a reporter cover the invasion. "Clemson's mechanized army rolled through the foothills of the Piedmont today, sweeping before it all attempts at defense in the buffer states of Pendleton, LaFrance and Sandy Springs, and marched triumphantly into the heart of Anderson on the minute of a pre-arranged schedule," his article read. The *Daily Mail* prefaced the piece by saying, "Following is the last in a series of 'propaganda' stories published by the *Independent* and the *Daily Mail* to furnish a realistic background for fifth column maneuvers staged in the city late yesterday afternoon. The harmless 'capture' of Anderson took place shortly after 7:30 p.m. and the *Daily Mail* a few minutes later issued a dictator-censored 'extra' reporting the events as newspapers in conquered European countries have been forced to report the subjugation of the people."

The paper read like an American citizen's worst nightmare. "You who obey the directions given in this Proclamation and our other orders and ordinances have nothing to fear from the Army of the ROTC and will be protected by it. YOU WHO FAIL TO RENDER SUCH OBEDIENCE OR WHO COMMIT CRIMES OR OFFENSES WILL BE SEVERLY PUNISHED." Pictures in the special edition were censored. Ads for churches and other subversive elements were blacked out.

At this time, World War II was in full swing. Germany had taken over Yugoslavia and was headed for Russia. German and Italian troops had invaded Greece and Crete. British troops had run to the defense of Iraq to save oil in the region. British code breakers received an Enigma machine and began to crack Germany's previously unbreakable code. British forces had sunk the German battleship *Bismarck*.

On July 9, two days before the "attack" on Anderson, Soviet forces in Minsk, Bialystok, Volkovysk and Brest-Litovsk fell to German forces advancing on a former ally.

In Anderson and around the country, the war was something other people were fighting, but it was still the source of a fear that hung in the air. An estimated fifteen thousand people from the Anderson area and beyond came to witness the invasion. The newspapers described witnesses' reactions to the events as "certain it was something they never wanted to see happen."

After a few hours of invasion, the Clemsonian army retreated, leaving Anderson to fend for itself, a free and sovereign town once again.

And because it was the last day of the training for the ROTC students, it also meant dance time. The 1,350 students, Clemson officers and Anderson leaders who helped with the event were all invited to a "gigantic dance and celebration in their honor," according to the *Greenville News*.

Covered by newspapers across the country, the invasion was seen as a good training exercise for military cadets, but it was also a reminder of what could happen here.

By the end of the year, Japan would bomb Pearl Harbor, propelling America into the war.

16
The Marshall Orr House and the Orr Brothers

While Sam and Bill Orr both grew up in Anderson, they went on to live very different lives. Even so, their reunion at the end of World War II after several years apart was one few know about. Both men served exemplary lives of adventure and service, formed, some say, by their time here in Anderson.

First, a little background on the Orr family.

Sam and Bill Orr were the great-grandsons of Lawrence Orr of Anderson, a towering figure in nineteenth-century South Carolina. He had served as Speaker of the House of Representative in Washington, D.C.; had formed Orr's Rifles, the first military unit of the Confederacy; and was elected governor of South Carolina, the first Republican after Reconstruction to take the office. He was subsequently named ambassador to Russia by President Ulysses S. Grant.

His son, Dr. Samuel Marshall Orr, built the Orr House on Market Street in 1883. A home to him and his family, it is a smaller copy of the house his father built, called Arlington Place. Dr. Orr called his house Little Arlington. He practiced medicine in Anderson and went on to become an officer in local, state and national medical associations. He also formed a partnership with E.P. Sloan to create Orr and Sloan Druggist, a drugstore on Main Street in Anderson.

Dr. Orr was also one of the men who championed electricity in Anderson. After his retirement from medical practice, Dr. Orr served as president and treasurer of Anderson Water, Light and Power Company, which would go on to be part of Duke Energy.

Little Arlington served as a home to the Orr family until 1905, when Mr. and Mrs. Rhett Parker purchased it. They lived in the house until 1925, when the four acres of property and house were sold to Helen Hammett Orr, wife of Marshall Orr, Dr. Samuel Orr's nephew. The Marshall Orr family bequeathed the property to the Anderson County Woman's Club in 1973. The house now stands as the club's headquarters and is filled with many antiques passed to the club by the Orr family. The club works tirelessly to preserve and maintain the building while continuing to rent it out for weddings, special events and get-togethers.

Mr. Orr, in leaving the property to the club, was hopeful that the club could continue to make an impact on Anderson County, as it has for generations. The Orr family also continued to make an impact on the county. Sam and Bill Orr were brothers—sons of Marshall Orr Jr.—who had moved to Anderson during the Great Depression. Both graduated from Boys' High School in Anderson. Both attended Clemson, and both served during World War II. But that is where their similarities end.

The Orr brothers were often enterprising young men. At an early age, Sam and Bill started a magazine route and later sold light bulbs to make the most of Anderson's status as the "Electric City."

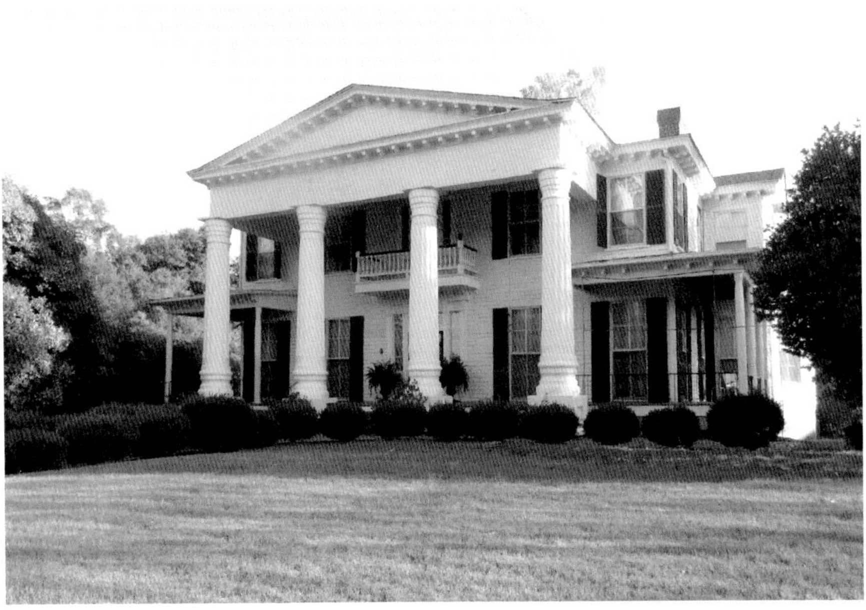

The Marshall Orr House. *Author's collection.*

Sam, the elder by four years, graduated from Clemson University with a degree in electrical engineering. He became a reserve officer in the U.S. Army and took a job with General Electric in Schenectady, New York, in engineering. He later moved south to Winston-Salem, North Carolina, and worked for Duke Power.

In 1940, he was asked to accept his commission and went to work as a White House aide to President Franklin Roosevelt. The country was watching and waiting for war, as Germany had invaded Poland in September 1939. Many believed that the United States entering the war was only a matter of time.

In the White House, Orr helped set up a battlefield "situation room," with maps covered in plastic so that generals could monitor troop movements.

The United States entered the war in December 1941, following the surprise attack by the Japanese on Pearl Harbor. Sam was asked to join a secret assembly of men who would be working as part of the British-American task force to decipher the Germans' coding system, known as "Enigma." Orr was sent to Bletchley Park, England, where he was assigned to General Omar Bradley.

There, he joined a wide variety of code-breaking experts to go through each German message to try to decipher Enigma's coding. Enigma created a "polyalphabetic substitution cipher," meaning that it created a series of letters to substitute for other letters. No letter could represent itself, though. Depending on the complexity of the cipher, Enigma could generate 150 *trillion* different letter combinations.

Still, the British and Americans were able to crack the code—but no one knew about it. British prime minister Winston Churchill ordered those involved to not divulge that the Enigma ciphers had been broken or that they were even working on the project. Sam Orr kept his word; the secret remained safe with him. In 1975, thirty years after Churchill's order, word of the project and its successes leaked out. In subsequent years, several books, as well as the 2014 film *The Imitation Game*, were produced.

Sam Orr moved on to the battlefield with General Bradley, seeing action across the European theater of operation. After Germany surrendered, Lieutenant Colonel Sam Orr was sent to the Philippines.

Bill Orr was successful, like his brother, but much more introspective. He also graduated from Boys' High School and went on to Clemson University. But after a year, Bill went to the United States Military Academy at West Point. He graduated as a second lieutenant and went to work with the U.S. Army Corps of Engineers in Los Angeles.

Bill also went to war. But instead of the White House and Bletchley Park, he went directly to the Philippines. There, he was assigned to the Fourteenth Engineers unit. Stationed in Manila, he was promoted to military intelligence and served there with logistics, civil affairs and military government until the fall of Bataan on April 9, 1942.

Bill and his men were part of the infamous Bataan Death March. After Manila fell to the Japanese on April 9, some sixty thousand to nintey thousand Filipino and American prisoners of war were forced to march from Mariveles and Bagac to Bataan, some sixty-five miles away. Many were not given food or water. All were marched without rest until they arrived at their new prison camp. Once they arrived in Bataan, the prisoners were forced to live in horrible conditions.

Bill showed his leadership in the prisoner-of-war camp, fellow soldiers said. In letters to his parents, officers said Orr provided other prisoners and his men with a positive attitude to bolster their morale, as well as taking beatings and humiliation for them, so that his men wouldn't have to suffer. After more than three years of suffering, Bill Orr and his men were released after the bombing of Hiroshima and Nagasaki, at which time Japan surrendered.

Sam found out that his brother was a prisoner of war in the Philippines when he got there in 1945. But he was unable to find him. Later, Sam saw the sporadic fighting in Japan between the time Japan surrendered and the time it officially signed peace treaties. He learned during this time that his brother had survived the POW camp. Then, in October 1945, Sam returned to Anderson to visit family and friends. To his surprise, his brother Bill was there, too, having recently arrived from San Francisco. The two met in the Marshall Orr house and spent time reuniting with each other.

After the war, Sam went to work at Hanes Hosiery. There, he invented a machine that made hose without seams and hose that wouldn't run. His wife was the first woman to wear non-seamed hose in Anderson. Later, Sam also invented the ever-popular L'eggs egg, a unique container for pantyhose.

Bill Orr received the Bronze Star for his meritorious service at the prison camp. After being freed, he was hospitalized for various diseases he had caught in the camp. In September 1945, he returned to school to earn his master's degree in civil engineering. By 1947, he had taken a staff position at the University of Minnesota, where he was able to flex his engineering muscles.

But he wasn't done with the military just yet. He decided that he wanted to be an airborne trooper. He took private parachuting lessons to get the proficiency he needed. On August 23, 1950, he parachuted from a plane at about 1,800 feet as part of his training in St. Paul, Minnesota. As he was

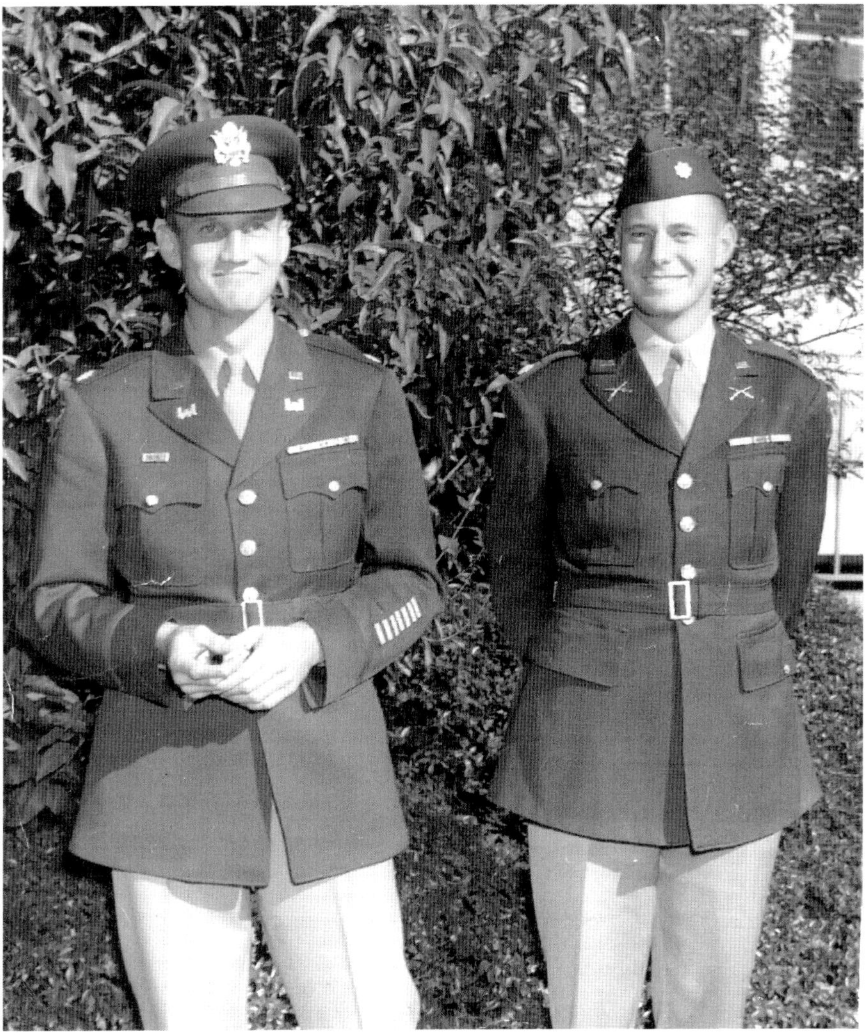

Sam and Bill Orr. *Courtesy Anderson County Museum.*

falling, a gust of wind caught him. He was blown into the Mississippi River, landing in the water, tangled in the cords of his parachute. Bill Orr died of drowning that day.

According to his sister Martha Orr Davenport, his one wish was to be cremated and scattered over Manila Bay. His mother objected, insisting that he be buried in Anderson. Since he had never married, his body was flown back to Anderson, where he was interred in Silver Brook Cemetery.

17

A March on the Post Office

While Anderson was ahead of some areas in terms of civil rights, the area wasn't immune to protests regarding this issue.

Civil rights concerns started long before the turbulent 1960s. In fact, as early as 1948, it was clear that civil rights was a divisive issue on the national landscape. In 1941, during World War II, President Franklin Roosevelt issued executive order 8802, which directed that African Americans be accepted into job-training programs in defense plants, and banned defense contractors from discriminating against African Americans. The order also further established the Fair Employment Practices Commission (FEPC).

When the war ended, President Harry Truman, under pressure, allowed Congress to end the FEPC. But in December 1946, Truman created the President's Commission on Civil Rights to "recommend more adequate means and procedures for the protection of civil rights of the people of the United States." The commission's 1947 report, "To Secure These Rights," made several proposals, including anti-lynching and anti–poll tax laws, a permanent FEPC and a strengthening of the Department of Justice's civil rights division.

In 1948, Truman urged Congress to enact all of the report's recommendations. Southern senators immediately threatened to filibuster. Truman acted on his own and signed executive orders that would beef up the Department of Justice's civil rights division, appoint the first African American judge to the federal bench, put several other African Americans in high-ranking administrative positions and abolish segregation in the armed forces.

Executive Order 9981 read, "There shall be equality of treatment and opportunity for all persons in the armed forces without regard to race, color, religion or national origin." Although the military resisted, by the end of the Korean War, the services were completely integrated.

At the 1948 Democratic Convention, a group led by Minnesota senator Hubert Humphrey proposed that the Democratic Party's platform include civil rights planks that included racial integration and the reversal of Jim Crow laws. Again, southern Democrats were resistant. But the planks were adopted; thirty-five southern Democrats walked out in protest.

Those Democrats formed the States' Rights Democratic Party, otherwise known as the Dixiecrats. Their party platform? Segregation forever, states' rights and freedom from government intervention to do business with whomever an individual or organization wanted to do it with.

At a convention in Birmingham, Alabama, the Dixiecrats decided on their candidates—South Carolina governor Strom Thurmond for president and Mississippi governor Field J. Wright for vice president. Their platform consisted of openly racist views held by many southerners at the time—opposing abolition of the poll tax and endorsing segregation and "racial integrity" of each race. Thurmond traveled the country labeling Truman's civil rights initiatives as "the most astounding presidential message in political history" and campaigning on states' rights and a thinly disguised stance of white supremacy.

November's election brought the candidates a defeat, but Thurmond carried the states of Alabama, Louisiana, Mississippi and South Carolina. While the party didn't win the election, it did receive more than one million popular votes and thirty-nine electoral votes. Truman went on to win the election with 51 percent of the vote. The Dixiecrats got 2.5 percent.

The Dixiecrats folded back into the Democratic Party, where they felt they could have more influence, until Senator Barry Goldwater ran on similar policies of states' rights and racial integrity in the 1964 presidential election. Goldwater's brash, no-nonsense conservativism led him to do no better than Thurmond had done, but it opened the door for the solidly Democratic South to move to the Republican Party. In 1964, Thurmond switched parties, and many of his segregationist adherents followed suit. Disenchanted with the civil rights planks in the Democratic Party's platform, Thurmond made the public switch, with Goldwater in attendance, in the middle of Goldwater's presidential campaign. Accusing the Democratic Party of "leading the state down the road to serfdom," Thurmond said the party had "abandoned the people to become the party of minority groups, power-hungry union leaders, political bosses and big businessmen looking for government contracts and favors." The move came less than six weeks before the election.

Goldwater lost to Lyndon Johnson. Thurmond went on to become the longest-serving senator in U.S. history.

But by the early 1960s, Anderson was well in the midst of adopting civil rights legislation. As early as 1962, the city council, hoping to avoid racial disruption, adopted a resolution that would repeal an ordinance prohibiting the serving of meals to African Americans, a law already invalidated by the U.S. Supreme Court. But the council wanted to ensure that eating establishment owners would still have the privilege of serving whomever they wanted. However, the council did approve recommendations that local black citizens would be allowed to use the recreation center for special events and any special programs they might plan. The council also voted, without discussion, to consider hiring African American policemen and to form a new biracial committee to conduct studies and make recommendations to the city council.

Within a few months, for the first time in nearly a century, black patrons were served lunch at several lunch counters in downtown Anderson, according to reports in the *Anderson Free Press*. It was seen as the first step toward integration. Although there were one or two instances of disturbances, there was no serious conflict as young boys and girls entered stores, sat at lunch counters and gave their orders. On the same day, members of the Anderson Chamber of Commerce (as it was then known) met during its breakfast club to hear South Carolina attorney general Daniel R. McLeod talk about the 1964 Civil Rights Act, which would be the precursor to even stronger federal legislation.

The city made good on its promise and hired two African American police officers by 1965. Calvin Clinkscales, twenty-nine, and Randolph Morris, twenty-five, were hired by a forty-four to four vote by city aldermen. Until that time, Anderson was the only city its size in the state with no African American police officers.

In 1965, the hospital desegregated, and Anderson County firms said they would comply with the 1964 Civil Rights Act. The act required that companies of more than one hundred employees be integrated. Companies with more than seventy-five employees had to integrate the next year, and firms with more than fifty employees were required to integrate by 1967.

Schools integrated with no problem. Anderson police chief Parker Clamp said he expected no problems when seventy-three African American students entered seven formerly all-white city schools. Anderson School District Five trustees approved the black students to enter the schools: two at McDuffie High School, sixteen at T.L. Hanna, nineteen at McCants Junior High, eight at Kennedy Street School, eighteen at West Market Street School and three at Concord Elementary. But, each of Anderson's nearly twelve thousand white students was given a "freedom of choice," allowing them to decide which school they wished to attend.

On opening day, only sixty-one of the seventy-five students reported for class.

By 1967, integration was working, or so it seemed. South Carolina's textile plants, which at that time constituted 81.3 percent of the state's manufacturing base, were employing more and more blacks. According to employment figures, there were 23,700 nonwhites with jobs in textile mills, compared with just 6,357 in 1962.

Only one place seemed to be a sticking point for integration: the post office. While post offices across the country employed many African Americans in the 1960s, there was little room for advancement. In Anderson, there was only one African American man employed at the post office, and he was the janitor.

Roy Davis had been born in Anderson and left to join the navy. After his tour of duty was over, he returned to Anderson to settle down. At the same time, the post office was moving to a new location on the corner of McDuffie and Calhoun. The new post office was set to be dedicated on Sunday, September 7, 1969. African American Andersonians had had enough and decided to protest the employment conditions at the post office. The local chapter of the NAACP applied for a permit to march and set up a picket line during the day's festivities.

The NAACP's application to protest was noted in the *Anderson Independent Mail.* Interestingly enough, the notice appeared above an ad for radio station WAIM declaring "No Jungle Music."

When the local Ku Klux Klan learned of the group's decision to protest, it filed for and received a permit to hold a parade in Anderson the same morning from 8:30 to 10:30 a.m.

The *Anderson Independent Mail* on September 8 reported that some 300 people attended the dedication. Senator Thurmond made brief remarks and presented the post office with a flag. Little was reported about the protests except the following: "Two marches were precipitated by the dedication. In the morning, participants included four persons in Ku Klux [Klan] robes and 17 in civilian dress. In the afternoon, there were 320 Negroes with a white priest in the front rank."

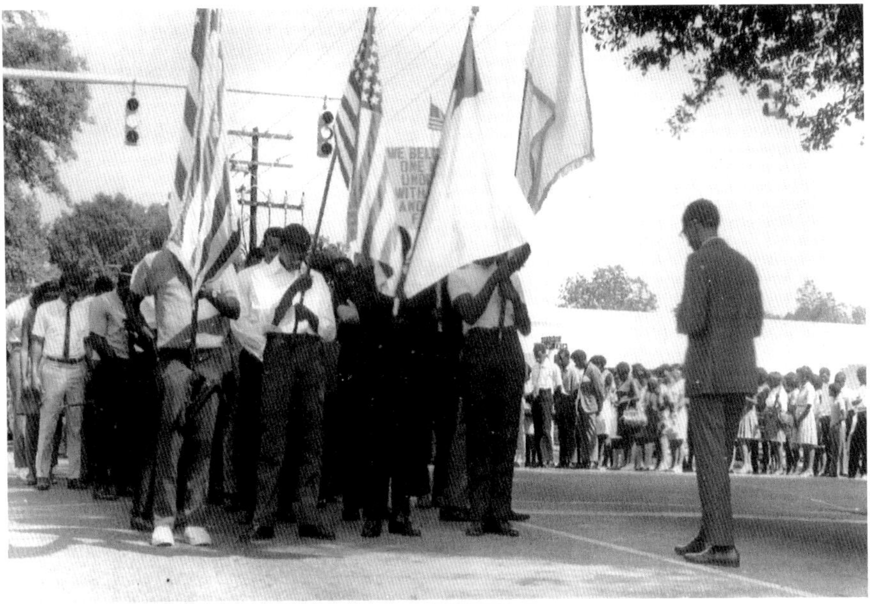

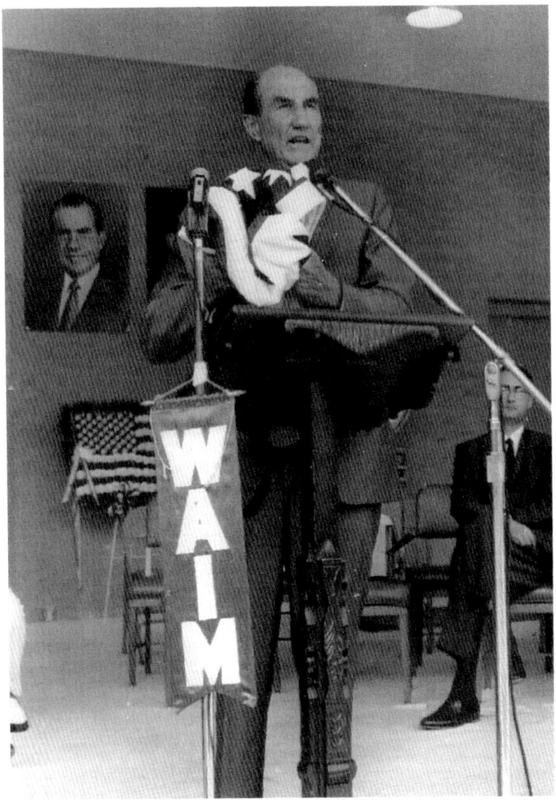

Above: African American protesters prepare to march on the Anderson Post Office's dedication. *Author's collection.*

Left: Senator Strom Thurmond presents an American flag to the Anderson Post Office during its dedication ceremony. *Author's collection.*

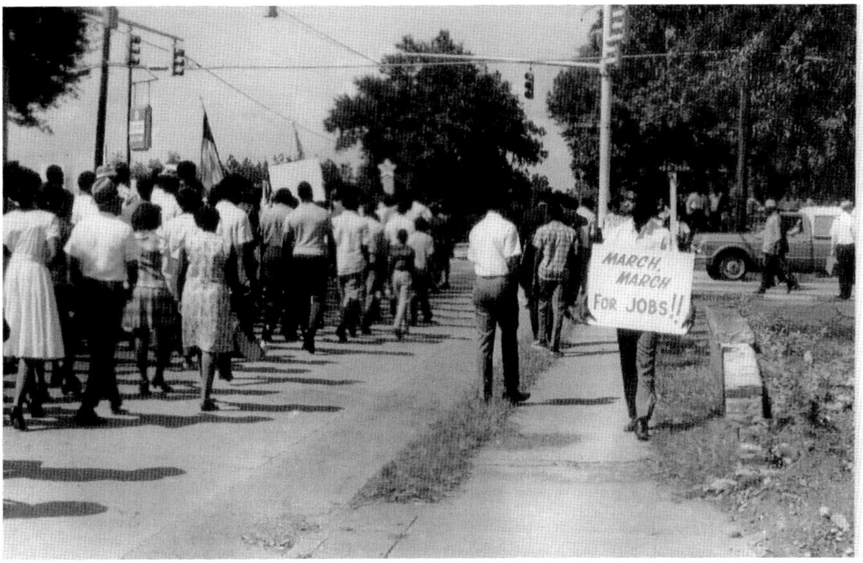

Protestors marched on the Anderson Post Office to bring attention to the fact that only 1 of the post office's 120 employees was black. *Author's collection.*

Whether or not the protest worked is unclear, but by March 1970, the post office had hired Davis as its first black postal carrier and postal clerk. Getting the job was easier than staying on the job, Davis said. Days started at 4:45 in the morning sorting mail. Delivering mail started at 2:00 p.m. and went until 4:30 or 5:00 p.m. In short time, Davis was promoted to window clerk—the first African American clerk in the office. Davis said he was subject to racism like he'd never seen before. "They'd never seen anyone like me in the window before," he said. "You could not imagine the things they said to me. For two or three years, I worked on the window. I took a job coming in at 3:30 in the morning to get off of it."

But still, Davis stayed. Despite racial threats and epithets thrown at him, he stayed on, even moving up to become the president of the American Postal Employees Union at the Anderson Post Office. For forty-four years, he served his country and his community—as mail clerk, mail carrier and finally vehicle technician—until his retirement in 2012.

Upon his retirement, he was honored by Anderson County Council for his service. Councilwoman Gracie Floyd read the proclamation, which said, in part, "Anderson County is fortunate to have citizens of vision and commitment, like Roy Davis, who step forward to lead and energize our community, often at considerable sacrifice."

18

Anderson and the Monopoly Scandal

Since 1987, McDonald's Corporation has given away millions of dollars during its annual Monopoly game. But for a five-year period, no one actually won the big prizes, thanks to a group of eight scam artists, several of whom came from the Anderson County area.

McDonald's Monopoly game is pretty simple. The company buys pull-off stickers that are given away as attachments to various food items. When you pull open the ticket, you have a chance to win a food item, prizes like game or computer systems, or even money—from $0.50 to $1,000,000.00.

When the game started, the company said it was giving away more than $40 million worth of prizes. Over the last decade, the company has given away more than $1 billion in the promotional games, company officials say. In order to do that, however, McDonald's orders more than 400 million pull-off pieces to be printed each year. (In 2016, McDonald's ordered 500 million game pieces.)

The game pieces are usually included on the containers for large drinks, large fries, Big Macs, hash browns and other premium items. Each pull-off piece is a property on the Monopoly game board, from Baltic Avenue to Boardwalk, and every railroad and utility company in between. Each of these pieces, in turn, has a prize attached to it. Pieces can be very common or very rare; in many cases, you have to get not only the common pieces but also a rare piece in order to win a prize. For instance, in order to win $1 million, you must get a Park Place and a Boardwalk game piece. According to McDonald's, the odds of getting Park Place are 1 in 11. The odds of getting Boardwalk are 1 in 651,000,000. Nevertheless, many people have won $1 million prizes. In 2010, a Wisconsin man, Jonathan Kehoe, won with his last dime—literally.

Kehoe, an unemployed construction worker, was using the last of his unemployment benefits to buy his nephew something to eat at his local McDonald's. At first, Kehoe said he wasn't going to get anything. After all, he'd been eating there a lot since he lost his job, mostly because the food was so cheap. But when he saw they had McRibs on the menu, he decided to get a meal. When the food came, he found the Boardwalk piece on his sandwich and the Park Place game piece on his drink. The odds of getting both Park Place and Boardwalk? 1 in 3.5 billion.

Because McDonald's is forbidden from administering its own game, it hired a marketing company, Simon Worldwide, to oversee the game. Simon was responsible for not only creating the game pieces but also for distributing them.

In 1995, administrators at St. Jude's Children's Research Hospital in Memphis, Tennessee, were surprised to open the mail and find a winning ticket inside of an envelope. No one came forward, and no one ever took responsibility for the action, so St. Jude's asked McDonald's for the award money. Although the rules state that the prizes are nontransferrable, McDonald's conceded and gave the award money to the children's hospital.

Six years later, the FBI received a tip that none of the big prizes were going to individuals and that the winning prizes were being diverted to a small group of people. The tipster told the FBI the scam was ongoing and wouldn't stop. When FBI officials looked into the tip, they found several references in their evidence and interviews to an "Uncle Jerry." This turned out to be Jerry Jacobson of Lawrenceville, Georgia, an employee of Simon Marketing who oversaw the security of the game pieces. The scam was simple. Jacobson provided winning tickets to friends, who recruited others to cash in the tickets. The recruits got a portion of the winnings and paid cash settlements to Jacobson and whoever had recruited them. The investigation centered, however, on Ronald Hughey of Anderson.

According to FBI affidavits, in April 2000, Hughey cashed in a $1 million prize he claimed to have gotten at a McDonald's restaurant in Tennessee. Hughey also claimed to have been a lifelong resident of Tennessee. His goal, investigators said, was to not raise suspicion on another winning ticket being claimed in the South Carolina Upstate.

When FBI investigators looked into Hughey, they found that he had gotten a Tennessee driver's license in March 2000 and phone service at an apartment just days earlier. FBI officials were able to use that information to stall McDonald's from sending out checks to Hughey and Brenda Phenis of Westminster, South Carolina. Phenis stated that she lived in Asheville, North Carolina, when she tried to claim her $500,000 game prize.

Using wiretaps, the FBI followed conversations from Hughey and Phenis to Dwight and Linda Baker, Phenis's sister, also of Westminster. In July, Hughey and Phenis called the Bakers to let them know that they hadn't received their checks from McDonald's. Dwight Baker, in turn, contacted Jacobson, who told Baker to masquerade as Phenis's son and threaten McDonald's with a lawsuit, or else they would "go to Burger King."

McDonald's released the check to Phenis in July. According to the deal the group had brokered, Phenis was to pay the taxes on the $500,000, give $90,000 to Baker and $70,000 to Hughey. But the Bakers believed that Phenis had taken the money and moved to California. Dwight Baker began to insist that Phenis give the Bakers the entire $500,000, threatening to call the U.S. Marshals Service if she didn't.

Linda Baker was then heard on the phone saying that Phenis was just the "front man" and that the ticket never belonged to her, but that she was being asked to cash it to keep suspicion off the Upstate. Dwight Baker told relatives on the phone later that night that the ticket was his and that if she would cash it and keep her mouth shut, he would give her $90,000.

Later that week, Dwight Baker met with Jerome Jacobson off Route 11 near Fair Play. FBI agents were able to stake out the area and watch the two men talk. Agents assumed that Baker paid Jacobson for Phenis's portion of the winning ticket and that Jacobson gave Baker another winning ticket to collect.

According to investigators, the scam started simply enough. Jacobson, a former police officer, was the sole man responsible for transferring the game pieces to manufacturers of McDonald's cups and other food containers. In 1989, he said, he stole a game piece worth $25,000 and handed it over to a relative. By the mid-1990s, he was taking all of the most valuable game pieces.

His method was simple, if not straight from a spy movie. While he was transferring the pieces, Jacobson would slip into an airport bathroom and open the envelopes containing the prize pieces, remove the most valuable ones and return the others to their envelopes for delivery. But since he couldn't cash the tickets himself, he would recruit friends and family members to do so. He would take more than fifty pieces, give them to his conspirators and then reap kickbacks in the form of cash. The conspirators would then mortgage their houses to pay off "Uncle Jerry" for his portion of the ticket while they continued to collect the prize money after he was paid off.

The Bakers had trusted, and continued to trust, Ronald Hughey. Baker, FBI agents said in affidavits, then gave the two final tickets to Hughey. Hughey recruited a family member, John F. Davis of Granbury, Texas, to claim the prize; the winnings would be split among Davis and the recruiters along the chain. Davis said he received two tickets. On July 30, 2000, he claimed he had received the tickets from two different restaurants in Texas, on July 24 and July 26.

On August 20, at 6:30 a.m., agents from the FBI staked out the Baker and the Hughey homes. By Tuesday morning, August 21, all three were arrested—the Bakers at 8:15 a.m. and Hughey at 9:00 a.m. Davis was also arrested on August 21.

Eight people were arrested initially in the scam, including Jacobson, Hughey, the Bakers, Phenis and Davis, as well as George Chandler of Walhalla. As the investigation continued, more ties to South Carolina were uncovered.

One tipster to the FBI said that a man in Charleston purchased a winning ticket for a car from a strip club owner. The ticket holder presented a game piece in Statesboro, Georgia, for a 1996 Dodge Viper. He said he had purchased the game piece from a man named "Dominic" who owned the Charleston strip club. The ticket holder then recruited his father-in-law to "win" a $1,000,000 prize paid in $50,000 annual installments. According to the scam, the winner would pay Jacobson $50,000 in cash, and the rest was theirs. The next year, the Charleston winner recruited two of his relatives, both brothers-in-law, to win a $1,000,000 prize and a $100,000 prize. Next, he recruited a Charleston car salesman to win a $1,000,000 prize.

Eventually, more than fifty people would be indicted in the scam that investigators felt had been going on since the late 1980s. The crime had robbed the fast-food restaurant of more than $20 million. The government asked in the criminal complaint for repayment not only of the money won in the scam but also of prizes, including a 1989 Mercedes Roadster, a 1995 Ford F350 pickup truck, a 1997 Isuzu Rodeo, a 1997 Lexus ES300, a 1998 Chevrolet Corvette, a 2000 Honda S2000 and a 2001 Toyota Highlander.

Jacobson pleaded guilty in April 2002. When asked why he had done it, Jacobson's attorney said, "He has reflected long and hard on it, and the only thing he could come up with was utter stupidity on his part."

Hughey and Davis pleaded guilty in 2002.

The scam had ramifications for the companies involved, as well. Within days of the scandal hitting the media, McDonald's was quick to point out that none of its employees had been a part of the scam and that the company would make it up to its customers. McDonald's then fired Simon Marketing. The restaurant's stock surged; Simon's tanked. By 2002, Simon Marketing was virtually out of business. McDonald's later sued Simon over the scandal. But in a legal twist, Simon ended up winning a settlement of $16.6 million from McDonald's, instead.

Two more interesting twists came out of the scandal.

It turns out that Jacobson was the one who sent the winning ticket to St. Jude's. The ticket was about to expire; without anyone to cash it, he sent it to St. Jude's in the hopes that McDonald's would honor it. They did and continued to do so when it was determined the ticket was obtained fraudulently. In addition, McDonald's decided to give away more than $6 million across the country to make good on its promises to customers.

One of the winners, Patrick Collier of Holly Hill, Florida, was a homeless man living with his fiancée and her mother in a hotel. Restaurant managers picked him at random from customers entering the store on a Saturday morning just after 10:00 a.m. Collier said that when managers approached him, he thought he had done something wrong. "I was confused when they handed me this certificate telling me I had won a million dollars," he said at the time. "I'm getting a Harley and a couple of houses."

Just months before, Collier had been living on the streets with his fiancée, Sandi Fabian, sleeping on cardboard boxes and making $50 a day as laborers when they could get work. Less than a month later, Collier was arrested for hitting and choking his fiancée and was arrested for failure to pay child support. His $50,000-a-year check from McDonald's was reduced immediately by the amount of back child support he owed, as well as repayments to the federal and state government for welfare payments made to his ex-wife because of his lack of support.

Hughey, Dwight Baker and Phenis pled guilty, were sentenced to three years' probation and ordered to make restitution. Linda Baker pleaded guilty, was sentenced to thirty days' probation and ordered to make restitution, as well.

In 2004, an appeals court overturned Chandler's conviction, citing "a complete failure of proof" that Chandler was involved in a conspiracy. The decision meant that he could not be retried for the crime and that the government could no longer order him to pay restitution for the amounts he had collected.

Jacobson pleaded guilty and served three years in federal prison. He was released in October 2005.

Bibliography

Abbeville Banner. "Johnson Female Seminary." January 25, 1851.

Anderson Independent. "Clemsonian Fifth Columnists Pave Way for Swift Occupation; Big Crowd on Hand for Blitz." July 11, 1941.

Anderson Independent Mail. "FBI Focusing on Real Winners." August 23, 2001.

———. "Permits Issued." September 5, 1969.

Anderson Intelligencer. "Aerialist Falls to Death." November 8, 1905.

———. "Andersonville—An Old Town Reminisences of the Past—Bad Guns etc." June 11, 1865.

Appalachian History. "The South Carolina Man Who Put the Electric in 'The Electric City.'" July 5, 2015.

Badders, Hurley. *Anderson County: A Pictorial History*. Virginia Beach, VA: Donning Company, 1983.

Beacham, Frank. *Whitewash: A Southern Journey Through Music, Mayhem and Murder*. N.p.: Self-published, 2007.

Brown, Harry. Acting Secretary of Agriculture. "Misbranding of Lifsey's Vim Herb, US v. 90 Bottles of Vim Herb; Default Judgement of Condemnation and Destruction." February 1927.

Charnov, Dr. Bruce. "Amelia Earhart, John M. Miller and the First Transcontinental Autogiro Flight in 1931." In *Autogiro to Gyroplane: The Amazing Survival of an Aviation Technology*. Santa Barbara, CA: Praeger Publishers, 2003

Dickson, Frank A. *Journeys into the Past—The Anderson Region's Heritage*. N.p.: Self-published, 1975.

Earle, Wilton. *Manse: One Man's War*. N.p.: Adept, 1996.

Ethridge, Roy, "Anderson County 1929–1972: A Chronology of Selected News, Events and Historical Highlights." *Journal* (Williamston), 2003.

Fenster, J.M. *Ether Day: The Strange Tale of America's Greatest Medical Discovery and the Haunted Men Who Made It*. New York: Harper Collins, 2001.

Glenn, L. Mell. *The Story of a Sensational Trial*. N.p.: Keys Printing Company, 1965.

Greenville News. "Anderson Man Pleads in Fast-Food Ticket Scam." August 15, 2002.

———. "8 Charged with Fixing McDonald's Game." August 22, 2001.

———. "18 More Indicted in McDonald's Scam." December 8, 2001.

———. "McDonald's Makes Man a Millionaire." September 3, 2001.

———. "McDonald's Plans New Game to Reassure Customers." August 15, 2001.

———. "2 Plead Guilty in McDonald's Scam." August 15, 2002.

Grose, Philip, "South Carolina at the Brink—Robert McNair and the Politics of Civil Rights," 2006.

History of Conklin Shows, "Definitions and Brief History of Carnivals and Midways," 2009.

Morton, Ella. "The Ether Dome, Where Everything Was Beautiful and Nothing Hurt." *Atlas Obscura*, January 8, 2014.

Oliver, Robert. *A Faithful Heart—The Journals of Emmala Reed, 1865 and 1866*. Columbia: University of South Carolina Press, 2004.

Orr, Martha. *Two Brothers from Anderson*. Anderson, SC: Anderson County Museum, 2010. Exhibition catalogue.

Otter, Richard. *Anderson County: Twentieth Century, Memories & Reflections*. Anderson County, SC: Friends of the Library, 2006.

Universal Pictures. "City 'Seized' in 5th Column Blitz Demonstration." Newsreel. July 1941. http://www.criticalpast.com.

U.S. Historical Marker Project. "Portman Dam and Power Plant." 2008.

Vandiver, Louise. *Traditions and History of Anderson County*. 1928. Anderson: South Carolina Genealogical Society, 2003.

Welborn, Gene. *A Town Springs Forth*. Williamston, SC: Family History Publishers, 2000.

Wells, H. *A History of the Discovery of the Application of Nitrous Oxide Gas, Ether and Other Vapors to Surgical Operations*. Hartford, 1847.

Wilhite, Dr. Wilson. "P.A. Wilhite and the Discovery of Ether Anesthesia." *Bulletin of Anesthesia History* (March 2011).

Index

P

R

S

T

V

W

About the Author

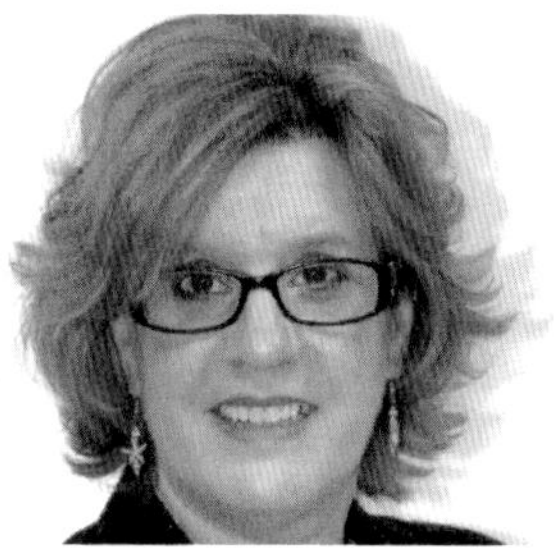

For the past twenty years, Liz Carey has been telling the stories of those around her. An award-winning journalist in Ohio, Kentucky and South Carolina, Carey has covered religion, government and education—and everything in between. Carey graduated from Miami University and cut her teeth in journalism, writing for *Everybody's News*, Cincinnati's original alternative newsweekly, before moving on to *Cincinnati CityBeat*, the Community Press family of papers and, finally, the *Anderson Independent Mail.* Originally from Versailles, Kentucky, Carey lives in Anderson, South Carolina, where she is involved with several nonprofit organizations, including the Anderson County Woman's Club, the Friends of the Anderson County Library and Anderson County Democratic Women. Currently, she works from home in a house she shares with a dog, two cats, two teenagers and her husband.